Christmas Spirit

COMPILED AND EDITED BY TERRI KALFAS

GRACE
PUBLISHING

Royalties for this book are donated to Samaritan's Purse.

CHRISTMAS SPIRIT

ISBN-13: 978-1-60495-085-4

From Samaritan's Purse

We so appreciate your donating all royalties from the sale of the books *Divine Moments, Christmas Moments, Spoken Moments, Precious Precocious Moments, More Christmas Moments, Stupid Moments, Additional Christmas Moments, Loving Moments, Merry Christmas Moments, Cool-inary Moments, Moments with Billy Graham, Personal Titanic Moments, Remembering Christmas, Romantic Moments, Pandemic Moments, Christmas Stories, Broken Moments, Celebrating Christmas, Grandma's Cookie Jar, Can, Sir!* and now, *Christmas Spirit* to Samaritan's Purse.

What a blessing that you would think of us! Thank you for your willingness to bless others and bring glory to God through your literary talents. Grace and peace to you.

Samaritan's Purse Mission Statement:

Samaritan's Purse is a nondenominational evangelical Christian organization providing spiritual and physical aid to hurting people around the world.

Since 1970, Samaritan's Purse has helped victims of war, poverty, natural disasters, disease, and famine with the purpose of sharing God's love through His Son, Jesus Christ.

Go and do likewise
Luke 10:37

You can learn more by visiting their website at
samaritanspurse.org

Dedicated to Yvonne Lehman,
who helped bring the Divine Moments series into being,

to the writers who share our vision,

and to the readers
we hope will be blessed by our stories.

Table of Contents

1

FALL ON YOUR KNEES

Constance Gilbert

M r. and Mrs. Santa (friends of our family) had invited me to their Christmas Eve Family Mass. The old church was decorated with evergreen boughs, holly, and red bows. Candlelight flickered in the stained glass windows. The organ played softly. Occasionally, a tiny bell would ring somewhere within the pews, followed by a parent's whispered, "Shh, not yet."

As I looked around, I saw children everywhere. Little girls in red dresses sat on Daddys' laps trying to see around the grown-ups. Little boys in Christmas sweaters wiggled and moved from Mommy to Daddy to Grandma and back. Older children tried to help with their younger siblings. All the children had small jingle bells on a red or green ribbon. It was hard to keep them still. Their excitement encompassed me.

A hush ran through the pews as the altar boys lit the candles. Father Fitzgerald entered and knelt before the altar; the choir began to sing. The mass had begun.

In place of the homily, a tiny Mary and a little Joseph slowly came down the center aisle. By the time they reached the front, a manger and bales of hay had appeared. Once again our attention went to the aisles as equally small shepherds with stuffed sheep and wooden staffs joined the nativity scene. As they arrived and knelt, I saw a baby doll in the manger. Last down the aisle, the kings-minus-camels carefully carried gifts adorned with jewels as they tried to look straight ahead and not lose their crowns.

Father Fitzgerald asked, "Whose birthday is it?"

The children yelled out "Jesus!" and Father Fitzgerald smiled as a few "Santa Claus!" mixed in were quickly hushed.

"I think we should have a birthday cake for our celebration, don't you?"

Immediately from the back of the sanctuary, heavy bells rang along with a hearty "Ho, Ho, Ho and Happy Birthday!" There came Mr. Santa ringing his sleigh bells and Mrs. Santa carefully carrying the birthday cake toward the altar. *All* the children's bells were ringing now!

When Santa reached the front, he quietly spoke to the priest while Mrs. Claus gently laid the cake on a small table. As she knelt at the altar, the bells ceased to ring so Santa could speak. I do not remember his exact words, but he explained about St. Nicholas and that Christmas was all about Christ. Then, giving a nod, he ascended the steps and knelt to pray at the manger.

'Twas the night before Christmas and all through the church it was silent. A violin began to play "Away in a Manger." The light dimmed slowly until only candlelight remained.

Father Fitzgerald prayed as the lights slowly came back on. Santa was gone.

The mass continued, but I don't remember any of it. Just like the children, I was awestruck when Santa prayed at the manger.

At the end of mass, families filed toward the doors that led to where cupcakes and candy canes awaited the children.

My Christmas gift came the moment my friend, Mr. Santa, knelt by the makeshift manger. He wasn't pretending to pray; he was talking to the Lover of his soul.

In remembrance of that sacred moment, every Christmas I place a figurine of Santa kneeling at the manger in a prominent place. I am once again in the hush of that old church as Santa walks up the steps toward the manger. I fall on my knees with him.

2

Frostbitten Nativity

Rhonda J. Dragomir

I'm the first Virgin Mary who looks like a Cleveland Browns linebacker!" I grumbled even though no one listened. I stomped my feet to see if the feeling had returned since my last stint outdoors. The blue nylon robe with a drawstring neckline fit well enough over my parka, but the hood underneath gave me a hunched back. I should never have checked my appearance in the mirror.

A live outdoor nativity scene had sounded like a good idea when the youth group proposed it. One teen's Aunt Minnie owned a farm along U.S. Route 48 a few miles south of Ludlow Falls, Ohio. Lit by thousands of Christmas lights, the frozen waterfall drew hordes of visitors from nearby Dayton. The frigid weather that year made the falls spectacular, their backlit columns glistening in the frosty air. The best road to the spectacle led right past Minnie's house, and our display in her front yard would be seen by hundreds of people.

Tonight, however, the needle on the outdoor thermometer beside Minnie's back door read fifteen degrees Fahrenheit. Players in the scene rotated in and out of Minnie's toasty kitchen heated by a wood stove. The first shift persevered for a full thirty minutes, but each successive crew shortened their time outdoors. Two hours into the six-hour schedule, none of the girls would take another turn as Mary. As the dedicated youth pastor's wife, I considered it my duty to be a good role model. I donned the costume again for a foray into the freezing night.

The snow crunched under my boots as I trudged across the yard. A glance into the night sky revealed thousands of twinkling stars. At least there wouldn't be more snow.

My husband, Dale, wrangled Jack, the donkey. Dale trusted none of the teens to manage the ill-tempered beast, which snapped at the fingers of anyone who tried to pet him. When I inquired earlier how they managed to get the donkey to our location from his home several miles away, Dale had muttered something unintelligible. I only understood the words, "pickup," "kicked," and finally, "you don't want to know."

Ignoring the chill, I flashed a warm smile at my long-suffering mate. His good humor made him popular with the youth, and he managed to make even the most onerous task fun. He returned my grin, his eyes sparkling more than the frost on the manger.

"Maybe I should go get into the Joseph costume." Dale's eyebrows waggled with mischief. "You are a hunk o' woman!"

I wondered what our guests would think if Mary smacked a shepherd.

I seated myself beside the manger, plastered an artificial smile on my face, and prepared to be pleasant to visitors despite my misery.

The roadside in front of the nativity scene seemed perfect for our purposes. There was no ditch, so cars could easily pull off the road and allow guests to stroll through our version of Bethlehem.

Jack was a big draw, but so were the sheep the guys had wrestled into the truck after the donkey disembarked.

Children swarmed the scene, their curiosity making for some tense moments. Dale warned them away from the donkey, but Jack drew them irresistibly. More than once, snapping donkey teeth narrowly missed their target as Dale jerked the bridle away from questing fingers.

The sheep were somewhat better behaved, but not much. They bleated incessantly and milled around in their pen, skittering away as children attempted to pet them. Their stench wafted right past the manger, and more than once I felt like I might upchuck on poor baby Jesus. I swore off more hot cider and brownies until the night was finished.

As I wondered how close I was to the end of my half hour, a disembodied voice broke into my thoughts, resonating over the plywood backdrop.

"Mary Kate, the man said don't pet the donkey. No, Mary Kate, you can't go in the sheep pen. Mary Kate, don't climb on the fence! No, Mary Kate—" The woman's shrill voice carried over the hubbub, and I braced myself for Mary Kate's visit to the manger. Feeling protective, even though baby Jesus was only my Chatty Patty doll, I lifted the bundle into my embrace and turned to meet the onslaught with my best imitation of Mary's glow of holy peace.

Mary Kate rounded the corner at a dead run. Stopping so quickly she looked frozen in place, she dropped the handful of candy canes she had filched from the bin beside the sheep pen. Her eyes widened and her jaw went slack. Mary Kate's mother appeared a few seconds later and plowed into her thunderstruck daughter, nearly knocking her down.

"Mama," Mary Kate said in a stage whisper, "is that really baby Jesus?"

The sheep stopped bleating for a miraculous moment and heavenly, perfect silence descended.

Mary Kate's mother offered no answer.

"Would you like to see him?" I invited the girl to approach, no longer fearing disaster. Wonder suffused her expression as she crept closer.

"He's sleeping now," I murmured, swallowing the lump in my throat. Unexpected tears froze on my eyelashes as Mary Kate reached toward the blanket.

"Can I hold him?"

"If you'll sit in my lap, we'll hold him together, okay?" My costume swished as I extended an arm to the girl, glancing at her mother for permission. She consented, brushing a mittened hand across her cheek to keep her own tears from falling.

Mary Kate allowed me to slip an arm around her slender frame and pull her up on my knee. She reached gingerly toward Chatty Patty, and I eased the doll into her arms. It wouldn't do for Jesus to take a tumble.

The child's blond curls tickled my cheek as I lowered my head to whisper to her again. "Shall we sing him a lullaby?"

Mary Kate nodded agreement.

Quietly, I crooned, "Away in a manger, no crib for a bed . . . ."

Mary Kate's words came out with little puffs of white breath. She only managed a few phrases with me. If she knew the carol, the words had fled her mind in awestruck wonder at holding baby Jesus in her arms.

When I finished singing, her mother interrupted our reverie.

"Time to go, Mary Kate. Give Jesus back to his mother."

Ever so tenderly, Jesus was returned to my arms. The girl slid off my knee, the slick nylon better than sled runners on icy snow. Before she left, Mary Kate turned and planted a sweet kiss on Jesus' forehead.

Exploding with exuberance, she ran to her mother, screaming, "Mama! I held the baby Jesus!" The child's wails of protest echoed off the backdrop as her mother dragged her back to their waiting car. A little heap of forgotten candy canes was soon the only sign Mary Kate had visited Bethlehem.

I think of that Ohio night when I see the nativity depicted on Christmas cards. Donkeys can be snappish, sheep may stink, and the stable might have been chilly that wintry night long ago. But in my mind's eye, one figure is always missing. On Virgin Mary's lap should be a little blond girl named Mary Kate.

3

A Wonderful Gift

Helen L. Hoover

Go ahead and open it, Helen," friends at the Bible study encouraged.

"Oh a music box, I love music boxes!" I exclaimed as the Christmas wrapping paper came off. The ladies in the group had heard me mention that I had a collection of music boxes.

Receiving a gift brings joy. It means someone is thinking of you and wants to give you something special. They are willing to spend the time and money to pick out the gift or to make an item they think you will enjoy. A gift is normally an expression of love and value for another person. Occasionally a gift is given out of obligation or to get something in return, but this is an exception.

The giver is thrilled when the gift is used and valued — whether it is a plate of cookies to eat, a new book to read, clothing to be worn, or a new item for a collection.

Other than salvation, the best gift anyone ever receives is the gift of who they are. God bestows this gift at conception. Each person is an individual with unique talents, intellect, and abilities intricately designed by our Heavenly Father. He is then thrilled when we use these abilities to glorify His name, help other people, tell of His greatness, and present Christ as Savior.

God has a plan for the use of our abilities. When we don't value our own gifts/talents, we can become envious of others, but as we seek God to learn how He wants us to use them, we realize not only their true value but also our own value. And when we choose to use our talents for God's glory, others will value Him.

Our combination of talents is uniquely put together by God.

You created my inmost being; you knit me together in my mother's womb.
I praise you because I am fearfully and wonderfully made; your works are
wonderful, I know that full well.

Psalm 139:13-14 NIV

4

The Christmas That Almost Wasn't

Barbara Latta

When our two sons, Kenny and Jonathan, were ten and six respectively, we lived in a small Louisiana town. My parents were in Arkansas and my husband's family was in Texas.

This particular year it was our turn to travel to Arkansas for the Christmas holidays. I knew my mom and dad would have lots of gifts under the tree for the boys, so I decided to let them open their gifts from us before we left. That way we wouldn't be hauling a lot of baggage in addition to what we would be bringing back from the grandparents.

I waited as close to the day of our departure as possible to have this early Christmas. We pretended it was December 25. Paper flew across the room, discarded ribbons filled the floor, and boxes were piled high. We ate the candy and the pre-Christmas dinner. Nothing except the calendar indicated this was not Christmas Day.

The boys enjoyed playing with their new gadgets and toys. They didn't mind opening gifts early at all. They had been begging to "please open just one" since the day the first package had appeared under the tree. They knew more awaited them in Arkansas.

Then the holiday balloon burst. The hot air of disappointment pervaded the room.

My husband, who was a Naval Reservist, received orders for a special short-term deployment that would start immediately.

Our trip went out the door with the wadded-up gift wrappings.

I contemplated making the seven-hour drive alone. But December weather in Arkansas is unpredictable, I would be traveling alone with two young children, and the route to my parent's house was filled with some backwoods country roads.

I decided the safe option was to stay home. I swallowed the lump that grew in my throat and had a good cry. How could I tell these two kids who had already opened all their gifts that Christmas was over for them that year? Yes, they had their stuff, but waking up on Christmas morning to a tree with nothing under it is not on a kid's bucket list.

I took a deep breath and wiped my eyes. The sooner I prepared them, the more time they would have to process the dilemma.

When I blubbered it all out, blank faces stared back at me. A few minutes later, Kenny said, "You mean we have to stay here? Will we have Christmas again then?"

There was no answer on my tongue at that moment. I'd already spent the gift budget. I couldn't go buy more. And also, Dad would be gone, so just the three of us would look at that bare floor under the tree on Christmas Day.

Of course, Christmas is not about what we can get, it's about what we have been given. Jesus gave it all. We celebrate His birth and the reason He came. It's just hard to get that past the disappointment that plagues a child's mind.

My reply was a faith statement. I had no idea what I would do. "We'll still have Christmas, it will just be a little different."

I dug deep and requisitioned money from various areas of our monthly budget in order to purchase some small, inexpensive items so the boys would have some kind of surprise under the tree. I put the borrowed bill money out of my mind and thought I would just have to find a way to make it up later. At least I hoped so.

I bought more food and snacks so we could have another holiday dinner. Dad's dinner would be a military MRE (meal ready to eat) out in the field somewhere.

In an attempt to recycle surprise, on Christmas Eve, while the boys slept, I also wrapped some of the gifts they'd already opened. At least they wouldn't know what was in the packages until the paper was torn off.

I faced the morning of December 25 with anxiety because I didn't know what their reactions would be.

My sons surprised me and also made me proud. They lit into the new, smaller gifts with as much enthusiasm as if they were opening expensive toys, and laughed when they opened the already used surprises.

But the clincher was when we read the Christmas story and they played with the Nativity set.

Jonathan picked up baby Jesus and said, "This is Jesus' birthday."

"Yeah that's why we have Christmas," Kenny replied.

Our Christmas that almost wasn't transformed into the celebration that was — and for the right reason.

5

Mrs. Claus Bakes

Theresa Parker Pierce

There's a kind little lady, I'd like you to meet.
She smells like cookies and candies so sweet.
She gives away chocolates and peppermints too,
for all the good things that the sweet children do.

She lives up north in a village of love,
where the snow-capped mountains can be seen from above.
She makes cupcakes with icing as white as the snow,
and rolls out fresh cookies from sugary dough.

She sifts, and stirs, and sprinkles each one.
She pipes and pours till the goodies are done.
For when they are ready, they'll go in the sleigh
for Santa's delivery, on Christmas Day!

Mrs. Claus wears velvet; her color is red,
with a fur-trimmed bonnet upon her head.
Her lips are pink. Her cheeks are rosy.
She makes the North Pole all warm and cozy.

She rolls out dough for fruit-filled pies,
blueberry, strawberry, and chocolate surprise.
Her hair is silver with soft pretty curls
that gather 'round her face like snow-white swirls.

Mrs. Claus is my sister, my mother, my friend,
my grandma, my aunt, my neighbor 'round the bend.
She bakes cookies with sprinkles in her nice warm oven.
She is the lady I'll always be lovin'.

So now boys and girls, you've learned the reason,
Lots of ladies today, bake for the Season.

6

The Rudolph Dilemma

Barbara Loyd

Rudolph, the fictitious red-nosed reindeer of Gene Autry's song, suffered a dilemma. Because of the way society treated him, he felt freakish, alone, unappreciated, and ridiculed. In general, he felt like he didn't belong . . . an outsider.

The truth is, any one of us can experience this. We, like the red-nosed cutie, occasionally will feel like misfits in our world because others make harsh judgments that leave us feeling inferior, useless, and lonely because we're different from them.

At times when these negative feelings engulf us, we must remember our Savior who comes to us during our personal foggy eves. He accepts us as we are and knows our potential because He is the one who created us and gave us that very potential.

Quite often, if we allow Him to, He uses us in mighty ways to shine His light in a dark world.

Consider famous outsiders from Scripture. Moses, Jeremiah, Daniel, Samuel, Paul, Peter, as well as Rahab and many others made a difference because they allowed God to use them.

God bestows grace upon those who are willing to use what He has given them. Whether it's helping to guide someone through a storm, leading others into the Promised Land, or being useful in some small way in our own community, each of us has a unique, God-given purpose.

God loves you and wants to use you, too:

Even if you feel you have nothing to offer as a part of His team.

Even if you are a victim of criticism.

Even if you are different from others.

Even if you have a shiny red nose!

The truth is, because we're Christians, we're called to be different. We shouldn't fit the uniform mold of the rest of the world. We should embrace our personal "red nose." And that might make us as feel as misfit as Rudolph did . . . until we, too, use that very uniqueness to help others.

God sees something in you that is often invisible to others. He sees His creation, His child, made in His own image, and whom He dearly loves.

So, whatever your red nose may be, become aware of God's grace embracing you this day.

Celebrate the fact that He has a unique job for each of us.

Who knows, maybe we, too, will go down in history if we choose to allow God to use us on His special errands.

7

Buffalo and Angels

Margaret Nava

W hy can't we stay home and watch Christmas movies?" Susan was annoyed because her mother had made plans to spend the day at a nearby Indian Pueblo.

"Because I promised my friend we would be there," Susan's mom replied. "Christmas is special to her and she's prepared a traditional Pueblo dinner for us."

"I didn't think Indians celebrated Christmas," grumbled Susan.

"They didn't before Columbus, but after they were Christianized, they adopted many European traditions."

"Yeah? Well, I'll bet they don't believe in Santa," argued Susan.

"You'll never know if you don't go," replied her mom.

* * *

Mom's friend Miriam and a young boy were sitting on a tree stump when Susan and her mom drove into the pueblo.

"Greetings, friends," Miriam shouted. "This is my son, Jacob. He will lead you to our home."

The boy jumped from the stump and started running toward the far side of the village. Within minutes he reached a small, earthen structure. Two bicycles — one without handlebars — and a wheel-less truck dominated the front yard.

Except for a large tin star suspended from the flat roof, there were no Christmas decorations: no lights, no Santas, not even a wreath. But once inside, Susan discovered a table laid out with red pozole, lamb stew, and Indian frybread.

After enjoying their meal, Susan and her mom followed Miriam and Jacob to the plaza where a group of men dressed in leather skirts and wearing buffalo-skin headdresses shook bells and rattles as they danced in time to animal-skin drumbeats and native chants. Snow began to fall just as several girls wearing white leather dresses and boots joined the men.

As the dancers' feet pounded the snow into ice, Miriam explained what was happening. "Every year, our people perform a different dance. This year, we are doing the Buffalo Dance, which recalls the importance of the buffalo to our survival. The meat of these animals became food; their skins supplied shelter and clothing; their horns and teeth were used to make tools and weapons. Nothing ever went to waste. Because the buffalo were so deeply respected, my ancestors watched over them and offered this dance as thanksgiving to the Great Spirit who created all things. When explorers came into our world they, too, received help from the buffalo even though they didn't understand our ways. Their priests taught us about the man named Jesus and how, on the night He was born, an angel appeared to shepherds who were watching over their flocks. The angel told the shepherds not to be afraid, *'I bring you good tidings of great joy, which shall be to all people.'* (Luke 2:11 KJV) Suddenly hundreds of angels appeared and praising God, they said, 'Glory to God in the highest, and on earth peace, good will toward men.'

"The priests wanted my people to give up dancing, and to

worship God the way they did. But instead of abandoning their traditional ways, our ancestors combined the old with the new. To this day, we perform the Buffalo Dance in remembrance of the buffalo and in thanksgiving for Jesus Christ who is more important to our survival than the buffalo ever was."

When the snow began to create small mounds on the dancers' shoulders, Susan's mom suggested going home before the weather got too bad. Susan furrowed her eyebrows and pleaded, "Can't we stay just a little longer?"

Have you ever felt so filled with the Holy Spirit that you felt like dancing?

8

Home for Christmas Again

Joann Claypoole

Home. It's where the love light gleams . . . ."

The truth of those words cut deep one recent Christmas. Several members of our immediate family couldn't join us for our usual holiday celebrations. The only visual communication were via Zoom or FaceTime. For the first time in thirty-something years, I didn't cook a ton of food, and we exchanged simple gifts two days before Christmas.

Two of our four sons donned surgical masks. One pulled a black mask up around his forehead. My husband laughed and said, "Are you trying to resemble Zorro?" Our youngest son, Noah, gave me a puny masked hug. "I'm sorry no one's coming tomorrow, Mom. I know how you love everyone to be together on Christmas Eve, but everyone's staying home for Christmas this year."

The only problem? They weren't *home* with us.

My husband packed our Jeep early the next morning and we headed north to our cabin in the mountains.

It seldom snows on Christmas in our remote, western North Carolina town. Yet we arrived from Florida a half hour before a storm hit without much warning. The Weather Channel's forecast had called for rain, not eight inches of snow.

"See, baby," my husband, Dennis, said, "God gave you lots of snow this Christmas Eve. It's His way of letting you know He loves you. He knows how much you miss the kids. Everything will be better next year. We'll all be together — right *here* in our tiny house."

"Home for Christmas? Here? Fulltime?" The thought of no more nine-hour drives north or south every few weeks thrilled me. And the concept of no more living in the furnace we call Florida boggled my mind. "Yay!"

"Now do you feel better about this holiday season being so different from our usual fantastic chaos?" He handed me a small gift box wrapped in red paper and winked at me when I held up the beautiful necklace.

"I love it."

A few days later, we celebrated New Year's Eve with bowls of chili and glasses of wine by the fireside.

"It's crazy," I said. "One of my fondest dreams will come true, but the world is still in the middle of a viral nightmare." While the realization we'd soon live in North Carolina fulltime sent my heart soaring, the mom in me worried about our family we would be leaving behind in Florida.

Two months later, in early March, I retired from the stylist/colorist business.

Isn't it weird how some curses are also blessings?

In some ways, living with a world-wide pandemic for over a year made the move easier. After all, Dennis's job wouldn't have gone remote if the dreadful pandemic hadn't spread and then recently resurged again.

The way businesses operated had changed over the course of

several months. Doors that had been sealed shut for years now flew open so Dennis could work from home. He slowed *way* down. And I knew that was a good thing — especially since he had suffered a heart attack a little over a year earlier, in January 2020.

"I'll still miss the children," I said, reminding myself how thankful I was to know our sons and their families promised to visit during the summer. "If I can't see our grandchildren often, we might as well be in Siberia. Wouldn't it be great if everyone moved here? Then we could all be together next Christmas. That would be my only Christmas wish."

"Sounds a bit unrealistic."

"That's why they're called *Christmas wishes*."

I envisioned our cabin bursting at the seams with kids and dogs running amuck. Snow-covered mountains add to the idyllic scene. Children listen to the age-old story as they huddle beside the tree. Laughter, song, and the intoxicating scent of Christmas cookies fill the air. All eyes bright and gazing as logs crackle and embers glow in the fireplace.

Dennis's nudge rattled me out of the fantastic daydream. "I'm not so sure *that wish* will ever come true. Let's take it one day at a time." He laughed and leaned in to hug me.

"It may take a few months to organize our own move from Florida," he said, and although his wisdom usually comforted me, I let out a sigh.

"Packing a huge house is so tedious. I wish we could blink and get on with living in the mountains."

A few months passed. We sold our Florida home before the daffodils waned in late spring. Our long-held dream became reality.

Thankful to prepare my hillside garden for summer, I took

off my baseball cap, and for a moment, let the sun caress my face. Tears streamed down my cheeks as memories of past holidays flooded my mind.

God, please let this crazy pandemic end. I pray for the day life will be normal again.

It had been too long since our kids and grandchildren had come to visit us. They all loved visiting the cabin for seasonal celebrations since we'd purchased the vacation getaway in 2016. The children enjoyed swimming in the lake, boating, tubing, hiking, and sledding — and trekking through my woodland garden, too. They also adored the decorations and lights we placed on the hillside every Christmas.

My husband joined in all the preparations. "I can't wait to see them either." He smiled and wiped a tear from his eye, too.

I grabbed handfuls of dirt and planted flowers while he flung three yards of mulch up the hill. After a while, I looked at Dennis and said, "Thank God it's almost over."

"So, we're done planting flowers? The priceless look on his face was worth millions. "I thought you loved gardening and never had enough roses?"

"I meant the pandemic, silly. It's like waking from a bad dream. Thank God everything will be back to normal soon."

"Maybe not so soon—"

"Anyway," I said, "I hope you're not right. Christmas is only a few months away.

After several weeks of long-awaited memorable family visits during the scorching summer, I focused my thoughts on God's grace, His unimaginable love for us, and how He's with us throughout life's challenges and storms. How strength comes from trials. And how my strength is only *in* Him. He's the giver of all of our seasons — good, bad, and ugly. He's also The Giver of life.

Labor Day was only a few weeks away when I pointed out that several people had been wearing masks while Dennis and I shopped at our local grocery store.

"What's up with all the masks again?"

"Haven't watched the news lately?"

"I hate the news."

"Huh?"

"My mother always said, 'No news is good news.'"

"She was right," he said and handed me the television remote.

"Oh no!"

For a moment, my thoughts turned inward. *How could this be happening again? And right before the holidays?*

But then I reminded myself about the incredible news we had recently received from one of our sons. "We're looking at houses online, Mom. We're moving up there before Christmas."

See, some Christmas wishes really do come true.

This amazing blessing came from out of nowhere. It reinforced the fact that no matter what we faced throughout the years, we always counted on God, one another . . . and yes, celebrating holidays together, too.

Although many things changed after the Covid-19 dilemma started, and the fate of future gatherings gripped a fearful world yet again, I believe God's plan is much bigger than this bug. His ways are much higher. Only He knows all our tomorrows.

So, with my thoughts on the manger, I will trust in Him today.

It came upon a midnight clear . . . .

Alone and unsure of the future, the newlywed couple awaited

the birth of Jesus, God's Son, in a lowly manger. The company of livestock and unseen angels stood in place of family and friends.

When I think about their reality and the raw truth of the story, a different perspective of any present loneliness calms my soul.

While I missed my sons and grandchildren, I imagined how Mary and Joseph's weariness and emptiness of going it alone through such unforeseen circumstances could have taken its toll. Instead, their season of solitude brought forth peace, joy, contentment, and deeper love. I was thankful for their example as we made the most of possibly celebrating Christmas minus the parties, crowded festivals, or lavish feasts.

Home for Christmas has taken on a new interpretation since the unusual holiday season when we were forced into quiet mode. The true meaning of Christmas, however, remains the same and rings ever clearer. It's time to remember and share the gift of hope. Whether it be via Zoom, Google Meet, or FaceTime, the essence of the message will never change.

We're not alone. At Christmas, or any other day of the year, God is with us.

9

The Chapel
on Christmas Lane

Becky Alexander

The Lord is in his holy temple; let all the earth be silent before him.

Habakkuk 2:20 NIV

Chapels top my list of places to see during road trips. I explore their history and take pictures of their design. If by chance I discover an unlocked door, I step inside for a closer look. A friend told me to make a wish upon entering a chapel for the first time and it will come true. Though I don't believe in wishes, I do believe in prayers. So, I send one up from each location.

On a trip to Frankenmuth, Michigan, I prayed inside the Silent Night Memorial Chapel on Christmas Lane. Everything about it fascinated me — the chapel name and its happy address . . . white, octagonal walls and a gold star above a domed roof . . . stained-glass windows proclaiming the Christmas message in vibrant colors.

The story behind the building intrigued me, too. In Oberndorf, Austria, Joseph Mohr, the pastor of St. Nicholas Church, penned a poem for the Christmas Eve service. He asked the choir director,

Franz Gruber, to add music. The two men debuted the tune on December 24, 1818, accompanied only by a guitar because the church organ was down for repairs. Today, the original Silent Night Memorial Chapel sits on the site to commemorate the modest beginnings of the famous song.

Inspired by a visit to the Austrian chapel, Wally and Irene Bronner constructed the Michigan chapel on Christmas Lane, near their CHRISTmas Wonderland store. In 1992, they dedicated the beautiful replica as "thanksgiving to God for His multitude of blessings."

Delights awaited me along a walkway around the chapel's exterior. Evergreens and lampposts lined the path. The familiar melody of "Silent Night" floated among the trees. Festive signs displayed the beloved carol in more than three hundred languages! My spirit swelled, while I scanned the words in various tongues.

PORTUGUESE (Portugal)
Noite feliz, noite feliz. O Senhor, Deus de amor.
Pobrezinho nasceu em Belém. Eis na lapa Jesus, nosso Bem.
Dorme em paz, ó Jesus. Dorme em paz, ó Jesus.

SOUTH SOTHO (South Africa)
Bosiu bo kgutsitseng. Tsohle di phomotse.
Ke Maria yo hlobaetseng. Le Josefa ya tshepahalang.
Bosiu bo bottle. Bosiu bo bottle.

We've shared the story of Jesus' birth through the simple words of a quiet song for two centuries now. The humble lyrics have provided peace and hope to countless people over the years.

This season, may we sing "Silent Night" with renewed focus, knowing its message has touched hearts across the continents.

> *Dear God of all the earth, we lift a gentle song of praise to You in English, Portuguese, South Sotho, and every language of the world. "Silent night, holy night. All is calm, all is bright. Round yon virgin, mother and child. Holy infant so tender and mild. Sleep in heavenly peace. Sleep in heavenly peace."*

The Greatest Gift

Norma C. Mezoe

Five dollars for a gift! It was almost too good to be true, but that's what my brother told me he had paid for my Christmas present.

I was born during the Great Depression when people struggled to make a living and the pleasures they enjoyed were either homemade or home grown. One of mine was popcorn from the crop Dad grew during the summer, and cold tomato juice, which Mom canned. We also enjoyed the vegetables and fruits Mom canned from Dad's gardens.

Dad was fortunate to always have a job, but often his salary was rather low. He worked hard, either as a mechanic, or a coal miner crawling around on his knees inside a damp, dark underground.

Few women worked outside their homes in the thirties and forties. Mom took care of the house and my brother and me.

We would probably have been classified in the lower income bracket, but since my friends were all in the same classification, I never thought of our family as being poor. Quite often, our clothing was homemade. One friend's mother sewed her skirts from colorful printed feed sacks.

Even though our income was limited, there was always enough money to meet our needs. But luxuries were few. That's why I was excited about my brother's gift.

My brother's gift appeared under our scrawny little Christmas tree the year I was ten. Each day before Christmas, I picked up the small square box wrapped in last year's smoothed-out paper and gave it a shake. What could it be?

Finally, Christmas Day arrived and I could at last unwrap that wonderful gift!

You can imagine my disappointment when I discovered a trinket worth far less than my brother had promised me!

In Old Testament scriptures, prophets of long ago wrote of a most precious Gift, which God would give to the world. This Gift is described in Isaiah 9:6 as *Wonderful Counselor, Mighty God, Everlasting Father, Prince of Peace* (NIV). It would be a gift of righteousness and unearned grace.

When this Gift, Jesus Christ, arrived He was all that God, through the prophets, had promised. Unlike my present of long ago, this Gift has an unfathomable price — free to all who will, through faith, accept Him. Romans 6:23 (NIV) tells us *the wages of sin is death, but the gift of God is eternal life in Christ Jesus our Lord.*

Five years after the disappointment of my brother's promised gift, I accepted Jesus Christ as my Lord and Savior. He has been all the prophets promised and I have never had any regrets.

As we rush about buying gifts during this beautiful Christmas season, may we pause to thank our God for His free gift of love and salvation. When we decorate our homes with tinsel, glitter, and pine-scented greenery, may we also prepare our hearts to welcome Jesus, the Greatest Gift.

11

Fan Ball

Pamela L. Stein

I t's Fan Ball time! My large, loud, and loving family loves to hear this on Christmas Day. Our favorite Christmas tradition is a game my Daddy named Fan Ball. The only equipment needed is wrapping paper and a ceiling fan.

Christmas mornings at Mama and Daddy's house are filled with family, lots of good food, and gifts for everyone. Almost all of our gifts are boxed and wrapped. No gift bags for us!

After lunch, the older children pass out the gifts. As they are opened one-by-one, the wrapping paper and tissue paper are dropped on the floor. The floor soon becomes a sea of colorful paper. When all the gifts are finally unwrapped and moved from the middle of the room, everyone grabs paper off the floor and wads it into balls.

It's Fan Ball time!

No matter how cold it is outside, we turn on the ceiling fan. As the fan spins, everyone takes aim and throws the paper balls up toward the fan blades. A mad scramble commences while the paper balls sail through the air. Those that fall to floor are picked up and tossed again.

Most of the balls fall to the floor having missed the target, but some make it and the fan blades bat them across the room. As those balls fly, everyone attempts to catch them. Some do get caught. Occasionally the fan blades shred one. Others catch people unaware.

The fan continues to spin. Wrapping-paper balls sail upward again and again. A whirlwind of activity fills the middle of the living room.

With paper balls soaring, shouts, laughs, and oohs and aahs get louder and louder. There is no winning or losing, only the pure joy of playing.

Eventually, the room quiets, the fan is turned off, and the whirlwind slowly disappears. The floor is once again a sea of wrapping paper — this time in the form of paper balls and shredded paper. The entire family flops into chairs and onto the sofa, exhausted by our Christmas Day tradition.

How often our lives can be like the Fan Ball whirlwind! We find ourselves moving in multiple directions with seemingly no purpose. The world bombards us with unending noise, senseless sounds, "paper balls" of stress that come from physical, mental, and emotional trials. We try to pick up the shredded pieces of a world full of angry people, confusing politics, and uncertain finances. Fear of an uncertain future, healthcare concerns, and loneliness add to the weariness of our lives.

It is difficult to find solace and comfort within this whirlwind.

It isn't until we search for Jesus, in the midst of the storm, that we can hear His words from Mark 4:39 (KJV): *"Peace, be still."* This story in Mark isn't only telling us Jesus was speaking. It is the account of a command from the powerful, omnipotent, sovereign Creator. The whirlwind instantly calmed, powerless against Him.

We can be assured that anything we face can be immediately calmed when we place it in His hands. Once we are willing to give over our trials, anxieties, and fears to Jesus, our spirits are instantly calmed. Those things become powerless.

We will always have troubles. We will always face trials. But we do not have to face any of them alone. We can remain calm knowing that Jesus, the one who has power over the storm, can take control of all our trials and troubles.

My family can control the whirlwind and chaos of our Christmas Day tradition by turning off the fan. Our Fan Ball game may seem silly to some. Yet it serves to remind me that only Jesus can control the storms of life. Only He can bring calm out of the chaotic whirlwind. Only He can turn off that fan.

At First Sight

Bonnie Lasley Harker

I think upon God's grace given,
In you, Jesus, gift from heaven.
His love formed this amazing gift
Who would souls save and spirits lift.

When Mary looked into your eyes,
Did she your purpose realize?
Or did she at first truly know
How far for her, for us, you'd go?

Surely it was love at first sight
That blessed, monumental night.
Amid acrid smells, dung and hay
With one look all faded away.

Roles of responsibility
Surely weighed down quite heavily
Upon your parents' trusting hearts,
Once realizing their true parts.

Did they grasp prophecy fulfilled,
And you from pain desire to shield?
It's not written within God's Word,
Clearly, what in their minds occurred.

I'm thankful for the grace given
In you, Jesus, gift from heaven.
For through you freedom came at last,
From sins present, future, and past.

Someday we'll look into your eyes
And too, will fully realize
The depth of love she felt that night,
When our eyes meet yours at first sight.

13

Christmas Keepsake

Susan Brehmer

M ost of the ornaments on my Christmas tree hold sentimental value. Some are passed down through family, souvenirs from childhood. Some adorned our tree as I was growing up. Others I acquired from craft fairs or Christmas markets. Additional keepsakes arrived as gifts. Many reflect my interest in music or serve as a reminder of an event, like the nutcracker ornament from the seasonal ballet I attended one year.

None came from school fundraisers. After all, how sentimental can a souvenir from a school fundraiser be?

Growing up playing violin and cello in the school orchestra meant participating in the occasional fundraiser to support the music program. Besides rehearsing classical music we held bake sales and car washes, and sold everything from candy bars to magazine subscriptions.

One year, we branched out and sold seasonal products including Christmas ornaments and wrapping paper. Equipped with a batch of catalogs and order forms, I sought friendly faces to see who would support our efforts and purchase an ornament for their Christmas tree. My customer base, close to home, consisted of family, neighbors, and friends, including a few from church.

A dear woman named Ouida — from my church — signed up to receive a symbol of the season. She and her husband were a kind older couple in our congregation who took an interest in me. I didn't know her husband well, but he often stood nearby quietly supportive, with a smile and an attentive ear. Ouida was the gregarious one of the two.

Ouida had a soft heart, an infectious smile, and a warmth that drew me in and made me feel welcome. Thoughtful and refined, she wore a suit jacket and skirt to church — her soft white hair perfectly coiffed — and spoke in a way suitable for a ladies' tea. Her manners felt a bit like southern hospitality. Each week I saw her at church she engaged me in conversation and inquired about my school activities and music. One year, she had let me interview her for a school project about what her childhood had been like decades earlier.

I played violin in church occasionally, and Ouida always offered sweet and encouraging words. Her support extended to the school orchestra when she accepted one of the ornament catalogs to peruse, along with the accompanying order form.

I let the couple know when I needed the filled-out form returned. As often occurred with school fundraisers, a long lead time followed the initial order request. The orchestra students gathered orders in the fall, but the seasonal gifts wouldn't arrive for a month or so after orders were turned in. A few days before winter break in December, the boxes showed up at our school. Next came distributing everything to the rightful owners before Christmas.

Since I knew I would see Ouida at church, I planned to deliver her ornament on Sunday. But a few days prior, my family heard word that Ouida's loving husband had passed away unexpectedly.

I felt terrible. After processing the sad news about her husband, my thoughts turned toward *now what?* The last thing I wanted was to bother her with something as trivial as the ornament she'd bought to support my high school music endeavors. I didn't want her to feel obligated or burdened to keep the purchase when she had other things on her mind. After all, she had simply made a kind gesture to support me.

Days before I would have seen her, Ouida called our house. After an exchange of greeting and condolence, she brought up the fundraiser.

"Do you remember that ornament I ordered?"

"Yes," I confirmed and paused. "You don't have to get it. It's okay."

"No, I still want it! My husband picked it out."

I had simply been selling an ornament for a fundraiser, not knowing I would be a conduit to making a precious memory. I don't remember the ornament — maybe a white dove? — but I do remember how Ouida's support of me became a Christmas keepsake for her that season.

14

An Angel Named Santa

Jennifer A. Doss

Some Christmases withstand the test of time and remain in your heart and mind forever, like the one we celebrated in a tiny mobile home when I was a little girl.

At nine years old, I was fairly observant and knew we were pretty poor. We never ate out at a restaurant and I knew better than to ask for my parents to buy me things if it wasn't my birthday or Christmas. Even then, my expectations had to stay small and inexpensive.

We lived in a mobile home located in a rural area outside Reno, Nevada. If you drove down our dirt road you passed others like it that dotted the landscape but were far enough apart not to be totally isolated.

The area was prone to cold, snowy winters. This year was no different. It had snowed several days earlier and the freezing temperatures ensured that the snow stuck around. After days of cars coming and going, kicking up dirt and mud from the road, the beautiful white fluff that had fallen was now more gray and brown. We'd have a white-ish Christmas, it seemed.

Our home was what you probably envision with the old term *trailer house*. Four large steps led up and into the front door. One step inside and you were in the small living room with an equally tiny kitchen just to the left. Beyond that a short hall led to the only bathroom and my parents' room. To the right of the living room another door opened into a room not much larger than a large closet where my brother, Jaime, and I slept.

Jaime was seven years my junior; our other brother, Jordan, was less than a year old. Jordan hadn't "graduated" to the big kid's room yet and still slept in a playpen in my parents' room.

On Christmas Eve, Daddy came home from work early, at around 7 P.M. He usually worked the night shift at his second job, but he had managed to get the night off and make it home to see us before we went to bed. Mom made a small meal and fed the baby while I ate and helped Jaime eat his dinner.

Daddy took a shower before eating and had barely made it to the kitchen when every light in the house suddenly went dark. Even the hum of the heater ceased. Frightened of the dark, we children began whimpering. Jordan dissolved in a full-blown wail. Daddy quickly found some candles and a flashlight and assured us that everything was okay.

Mom called the power company. When she hung up, she announced, "There's a power outage. They don't know when it will be fixed." She nodded at Daddy and they retreated to their bedroom to talk, leaving me in charge of the little boys.

We finished eating, hearing Mom and Daddy's voices rise and fall from the other room. When they emerged, Mom looked like she'd been crying. I didn't know then that the reason the power was out was because we didn't have the money to pay our bill, so the company had turned off our electricity.

I glanced over at our small Christmas tree with mostly

handmade ornaments, including the four I'd made each year since I started school. There weren't any presents under the tree. Mom and Daddy had already told me they couldn't afford gifts this year . . . but I knew Santa would come and we'd have presents in the morning.

"Tonight, we're going to have a camp out here in the living room," Mom said. She dragged all the cushions off the couch and laid them out. Everyone retrieved our pillows and all the blankets we could find — which barely amounted to one each. Then Mom layered the blankets on the floor to make a pallet and announced that we'd all sleep there together.

"What about Santa?" I asked, incredulous. Santa could not just walk into the living room where we were all sleeping. We had to go to our rooms.

"Honey, I don't think Santa is going to make it all the way out here." Mom said.

"Yes, he will. Santa goes to every house. Even the far away ones," I said.

It had been a hard year and adding a baby to the mix hadn't made it easier on any of us, but Santa had found us through all the moves we'd made in my nine years of life and he wasn't going to miss us this year.

Daddy smiled. "It's okay. Santa can come even if we're in the living room, I promise."

I didn't believe him but a chill filled the room and I realized the reason we were all sleeping together was to keep warm, so I didn't argue. Mom sent Jamie and me to put on footy pajamas, layers of clothes, and our warmest jackets while she layered Jordan's clothes.

Suddenly, there was a knock on the door. Jaime and I peeked out a window to see who it was. Daddy looked confused, like he wasn't expecting anyone. He went to the door, and opened it to find a jolly man in a red suit. I knew he wasn't the "real" Santa, because I could see the strings that held his beard in place and noticed the slight gap between the beard and his chin. It didn't matter though, I already knew Santa often had helpers who saw children in stores since one person couldn't be everywhere at the same time. He probably sent one of them tonight, too.

"Ho Ho Ho! Merry Christmas!" he bellowed.

"Santa!" I raced toward him and threw my arms around his padded stomach. "But we're not even in bed."

"I wanted to stop by early and be sure I didn't miss your house," he said, lugging in a large bag. He noticed the tiny Christmas tree and stepped over to empty his bag one gift at a time, carefully placing each one on the floor around it.

My eyes lit up at the brightly colored paper and seemingly endless number of gifts he lifted out. Of course, some would be for my brothers, but a few had to be for me. In reality, there were only around ten in total, but to me, it finally looked like Christmas.

When he finished, he hugged Jaime and me, but respectfully backed away as Jordan screamed in terror. I laughed. My silly baby brother didn't understand that this wonderful man had just brought us presents.

Mom handed me the baby and told us to tuck ourselves under the blankets while she and Daddy went outside with Santa. They were outside just long enough for me to get the boys settled under the blankets and sneak a peek at a couple of tags on the gifts. The biggest one was for me!

When our parents came back in, we huddled under the blankets and tried to sleep. Of course, I was too excited to even close my eyes. I just stared at the lovely gifts under the tree until I dozed off. Somehow, during the night the power was restored and we woke up to a warm, bright house. Everything looked and felt different.

To this day, my parents have no idea who the man was or how he knew to come. He refused to give them his name or any information. He just told them he was sent to bless our family. The gifts were some clothing and toys that were just right for each of us. And when Mom talked to the power company, our bill had been paid. I've wondered over the years if he was an angel sent to let us know we are seen, or simply someone who saw a need. I guess we'll never know.

I've always remembered that Christmas. And now, as a mom myself, I've often teared up at the desperation my poor parents must have felt that night right before a miracle happened.

The exact toys and clothes have long been forgotten, but the kindness and generosity of a stranger will live on in my memory.

15

One Shone Brighter

Linda L. Kruschke

"Gazing at a sky filled with stars,"
Wrote the Magi in his memoirs
"One shone brighter than the rest.
So onward toward that star we pressed."

He never says how many they were,
Those magi travelling with gold and myrrh,
But their destination he makes quite clear
Was to greet the new King who would soon appear.

The brightest star that rose in the east
Would guide them to One deserving a feast
But instead was born in a simple barn stall
And one day years later would die for us all.

"By the time we arrived the Child was but two,
And already we could tell He was holy and true."
I read this man's memoir and gazed up at the sky
Looking for the star that led the Magi.

All I could see in that vast expanse
Was the truth that it didn't happen by chance.
The Creator of each and every star
Led the Magi who came from afar.

16

The Bing-Bong Gift

Bonita Y. McCoy

Bing-bong rang out when I tilted the large box to the right. I placed my ear to the brightly wrapped package and gave it a little shake. The weight shifted, and a whirling sound like a quarter spinning on a table clamored from within the present.

My aunt had brought the gift to my house earlier in the week with the other packages for my family. Now, I sat next to the Christmas tree taxing my eight-year-old brain, trying to figure out what could possibly go bing-bong.

It couldn't be a doll, and it seemed too heavy to be a board game. Besides, the box was too big. My older sister had given me a pogo stick the year before, and even it hadn't made such strange noises. I tilted the box again, bing-bong, whirl-whirl, clunk as the weight shifted from one end to the other.

What could it be?

My mother picked that moment to walk through the living room on her way to the kitchen. She stopped and knelt beside me. "Are you at it again?"

"What do you think it is?" I held the gift tighter, and glanced at her.

"I have no idea, but tomorrow we will find out." Her eyes

grew wide, causing the excitement in my heart to stir. "But whatever it is, you've sure had fun trying to figure it out."

"Can I open this one first?" I pleaded.

"No, we have to wait to open these gifts when your aunt and uncle get here. And they won't arrive until closer to lunch."

On Christmas Day, I thought my aunt and uncle would never get there. I played with all my new toys and ate the candy from my stocking, but no matter what, the thought of the bing-bong gift wouldn't leave me.

At last, I heard a car pull into the driveway. My mom opened the door for my aunt and uncle and cousin, and all three entered, carrying dishes filled with food my aunt had brought for the meal.

The instant their hands were empty I begged to open gifts.

My dad acted as Santa and handed out the presents, one to Mom, one to my sister, and one to my cousin. Finally, Dad grabbed the bing-bong gift.

My heart raced. I'd waited all week to unwrap the mystery of those crazy noises. I'd shaken the package until Mom threatened to put it away. And now, it was time to see what was inside.

I slid my hand under the tucked edges of the colored paper and ripped, revealing an oversized shirt box. I pulled at the top to open it, but several pieces of tape secured both sides. Dad helped, and together we wiggled off the top.

There inside was a beautiful Holly Hobby quilt, a broken piece of brick, and a small handheld game that contained a marble and chutes. When you tilted the game, it made the bing-bong noise and then whirled.

Surprised, I burst out laughing. What a wonderful way to make the gift fun. Later, I asked my aunt how she had thought of the joke. She pointed to my cousin and said it had all been his idea.

That year, my cousin and aunt gave me one of the greatest gifts I've ever received: the gift of anticipation. Don't get me wrong. I loved the quilt and I still have it, but their gift of anticipation transformed that Christmas into a magical time, a moment so sweet I'll never forget it.

17

Christmas on My Grandparents' Farm

Beverly Robertson

Sloshing through the snow, our family car made it to my grandparents' farm two hours away. Ours was the only vehicle to have plowed its way up the driveway.

My dad drove to the front door and my brother and I jumped out. Grandmother ran to meet us, then pulled us into her warm kitchen heated by an old, wood cook stove. After shedding our coats, we scurried into the dining/living room to greet my grandfather — who sat in a big chair with large wooden arms — with gentle hugs because he had not been well.

Their old house seemed so fascinating. Later in the day, Grandmother said we could go into the parlor, normally off limits, to see a little Christmas tree decorated with simple homemade snowflakes, painted thread spools, and yarn balls.

As the daylight waned, Grandmother placed an old-fashioned, kerosene lamp in the center of the dining room table. Intrigued, my brother and I watched as she removed the glass chimney and lit the cotton wick. It was quite a novelty compared to our electric lights at home. We basked in its warm glow and made faces in the mirror behind the table, which annoyed my mother to the point of putting a towel over the offending object. Maybe we were so unruly because we had to wait until the next morning to open our presents.

After supper, it was time for bed. We visited the outdoor privy and then climbed the steps to our mother's old room. Mom kissed us goodnight and listened to our prayers.

As sleep eluded me, I studied several displays of her butterfly collection that hung on the wall. She said she had caught these beautiful creatures with a net, mounted, and framed them.

We finally closed our eyes and woke to the smell of something yummy wafting up the stairs. Grandma's delicious buckwheat pancakes were the only thing that made it worth the delay to opening our gifts. We hurriedly dressed and descended the steps where Grandma was waiting with her delightful, bear hugs. She and Mom had the table waiting with flapjacks and applesauce. Grandpa cut three stacks of cakes crisscross style, and smothered them with honey.

After the table was cleared, we finally could open our gifts. Each of us received two items. I recall admiring a pretty tin can decorated with wrapping paper. A beautifully crocheted miniature green wreath with red berries woven into it graced the top of the package. After lifting this little decoration, I was delighted to find the canister filled with dark chocolate fudge. My other present was a flipbook of an alphabet and animals. My grandmother had been a teacher, so maybe her background came through in this.

Our visit ended the day after Christmas, but we transported the love given to us all the way home, and it lasted until the next trip to the farm.

We shared a lot of Christmases with my grandparents. After all of the Christmases I spent with them, those two simple items are the ones that have remained in my mind.

Because my mother was an only child, we were the recipients of all our grandparents' affection. Looking back, I now understand just how much caring came from that humble farmhouse.

18

She's Canceling Christmas

Donna Collins Tinsley

The angels were alarmed,
"There's another mom on the edge.
She's ready to leave everything and everyone.
What can we do?
Lord, is it really true?
She's canceling Christmas this year!"

Yes, I'm canceling Christmas this year!
Why have it
When there's so many tears?
Why try to pretend
It will be good at the end?
Yes, I'm canceling Christmas this year.

Makes me sadder than sad ever was
It's Christmas but not the night that 'Twas.

If you knew all the pain,
You'd cancel it too.
Looking for light
And the Lord
Hasn't come through.

Makes me sadder than sad ever was
It's Christmas but not the night that 'Twas.

The world thinks Christmas
Is all about them.
Many people are
Consumed with
Rushing about,
Buying and wanting gifts
While heartache abounds.

Living life through a phone
Instead of talking
With those nearby.
How will they feel when they're gone?
One day they'll wish
That conversation
Had lingered on.

Makes me sadder than sad ever was
It's Christmas but not the night that 'Twas.

This mom just got tired
Of the constant strife
She just needed a break
From her own "real life."

Her tears stormed heaven
As a trumpet song given.
A battered, wounded sound
Came as she lay prostrate
On the ground.
Then the Lord was pleased
With her battered worship to Him.
He put a crew of angels to work right then.

One angel sent a song.
Another sent a friend with hugs.
One sent a book
For a fiction vacation,
A temporary
Break from this world.

Back when angels came singing,
Jesus was bringing
Hope for a deep, dark world.
The enemy roars,
But he won't win any more;
 Angels are surrounding the door
Of her simple abode.
They've taken this load,
Put her on a different road.

Prayers were given,
Because she's
Held up by friends.
The mom is renewed!

Now she's celebrating Christmas too,
Saying a Merry Christmas to you!

19

Just Like Mom
Used to Make

Margaret McNeil

My brother, sister-in-law, and nephew were going to spend Christmas with my family. This would be the first time we'd spent the holiday together since our Mom had died ten years earlier. I spent weeks poring over recipes, revising menus, and pondering how to make the day memorable.

As the last of the Thanksgiving leftovers were consumed, I still didn't know what to do. Drifting off to sleep one night, the answer became obvious. I would recreate the Christmases of our childhood.

Growing up on Guam as "Navy brats," my brother and I never had an opportunity to experience Christmas with extended family. The only thing we knew about a family Christmas came from watching episodes of our favorite TV shows. Mom knew what we were missing out on, so she used her culinary prowess to give us Christmases to remember.

As soon as December rolled around, Mom's tiny kitchen turned into a workshop. She grated Cheddar cheese, chopped pecans, and minced cloves of garlic before combining them with other ingredients to make cheese balls. She gifted the cheese balls, along with a sleeve of Ritz crackers, to friends and neighbors. Mom made sure to save one cheese ball for her family to enjoy on Christmas Day.

Once Mom finished making cheese balls, her attention turned to baking. She transformed flour, sugar, shortening, eggs, vanilla, salt, and a dash of nutmeg — her secret ingredient — into Christmas cookies. She decorated the cookies with icing in festive shades of red, green, yellow, and blue. She stored the cookies in the freezer, taking them out whenever we had company during the month. Mom also left a plate of the cookies and a glass of milk out for Santa on Christmas Eve.

To go with the cheese ball and cookies, Mom made a batch of holiday punch. She served the festive, red-hued beverage in her cut glass punch bowl, the base surrounded by a garland of poinsettias.

By the time we moved to the States, the big family Christmas was a thing of the past. Grandparents had died. Aunts and uncles had moved away. Married cousins now divided the day between their parents' and their in-laws' houses. Although disappointed we'd never know what it was like to celebrate Christmas with a houseful of relatives, my brother and I knew Christmas would not have been the same without Mom's cheese ball, Christmas cookies, and holiday punch.

So, when my brother walked into my dining room that Christmas morning, he was overcome with emotion. On top of the buffet that once belonged to our Mom sat the food from our childhood. A wooden board held a cheese ball surrounded by Ritz crackers. A platter overflowed with Christmas tree-, Santa Claus-, star-, angel-, and reindeer-shaped cookies. Mom's punch bowl was once again filled to the brim with holiday punch complete with a garland of poinsettias encircling the base.

My brother and I were teary-eyed as we ate the cherished foods and reminisced about past Christmases. It was an opportunity to introduce our children to the foods and memories created by their grandmother, a woman who died when they were too young to remember her.

Now that I'm a mother, I appreciate and understand why Mom only made these foods at Christmas. She knew not only was the tradition something for her children to look forward to, but something for them to look back on with memories that would last a lifetime.

20

On a Midnight Weary

Carol Smithson

Tossing back the covers, she more fell to the side of her bed than sat, feeling an exhaustion that permeated from her neck to her toes. Worry lined her face as anxious thoughts of a budget that would not balance and the fear of seeing disappointment in the eyes of her children peering under a sparse Christmas tree whirled in her head. Added to that, the expectations of others — and even her own — at this season created a dread of imminent failure.

What was this whole Christmas thing about, anyway?

She sighed, kicking off her slippers and rolling under the covers. Not having the energy to turn off her bedside lamp, she pulled the blankets over her head to block the light. If there was any time between closing her eyes and drifting off to sleep, she was unaware of it.

Suddenly a heavy hand snatched back the covers and an urgent voice next to her ear breathed, "Hannah, come quick! Something is happening!"

Her heart gave a wild lurch as she shielded her eyes from the light of a crude lantern. She jerked up, her breath coming in wild gulps as she sought to find her voice. Her chest heaved. She crossed her arms over her night gown, then looked down in surprise. The material under her fingers was a coarse weave. Her mind swirled with the shock of it.

"I'm not Hannah," she more croaked than spoke. The man had moved away, his lantern sending flashes of light around a small, square room with a dirt floor, a rough table, a few stools, and a loom in one corner.

What was happening? Where was she?

"Wife, hurry!" The man's voice was urgent. Wife? Her brain screamed *You are not a wife! Your husband left you years ago!* She blinked, trying to keep the room from tilting.

"I'm not married," the words rushed from her mouth, hung in the air. She lurched to the table and grabbed a corner of it, holding on with all her might. The man stood in the doorway; his lantern held high casting his shadow in relief. She could see someone approach him and she shrank back.

"Rubin!" exclaimed the man who had awakened her.

"Samuel, are you coming? The shepherds are all gone to the town center. They are searching for the babe as the angels instructed them."

"Angels," Samuel, the man who had awakened her, stepped back and his voice held, what . . . fear?

"Samuel, we must hurry or we'll miss it!"

"Aye. I'm coming. Just let me get Hannah. She has prayed for this all her life."

"I'm not married," she uttered the words again, shock clear in her voice.

"Hannah," Samuel came up to her with laughter in his voice. "Not married? And me providing for you these past thirty years. I think not, my girl. Well and truly married we are. Now come."

He slung a woven shawl over her shoulders, his roughened hand grabbing hers as he propelled her out into the night. She glanced up at the sky and stumbled in amazement at the number of stars shining in the night sky. She would have stopped to stare, but others were rushing past and she was afraid of being knocked over.

Her hand still firmly in — what was his name, Samuel? yes — Samuel's grasp, she reached up and grabbed his well-muscled arm with her other hand. They almost flew down the worn path. Other people hurrying from between tiny block houses all converged on their path as well. Ahead, a small village nestled at the base of a number of hills.

Though her brain continued reeling, she became aware of snatches of conversation.

"The shepherds came from the fields."

"Watching over the sacrificial herd."

"My brother saw them fallen on their faces."

"It was a bright light . . . ."

"Timotheus said they saw angels!"

Winded, Samuel moved off of the path to catch his breath.

"Where," she faltered, "where are we going?"

"To see the babe," someone volunteered, hurrying past.

Something niggled in her brain. Something familiar.

"Samuel, old friend," came another voice. A stooped, elderly man held a lantern as well and crowded beside them to get off the path himself.

"What have you heard of this?"

"Little. Probably no more than you."

Samuel's voice rumbled. "Shepherds came shouting down

the path. Something about seeing angels and being told to go see a newborn baby."

"Aye," grunted the other man, their lanterns showing rough clothing and sandaled feet. She looked down at her own feet, bare with what looked to be deep callouses.

"The angels said, 'Glory to God in the highest.'" A note of wonder was in his voice, and both nodded. "You know what that may mean . . . ."

"You mean the Messiah? Here? Now?"

"In Bethlehem?" her Samuel returned. Her Samuel? For a second her brain threatened to fold like a pickle, then the story clicked into place making her gasp.

"Come wife. We go to see this thing." Samuel pulled at her hand still clasped in his. She willingly followed now, her hurried footsteps matching his. They were swept along with the crowd until it stopped suddenly, melding with other watchers encircling a small house.

They stood on the outskirts of the circle. The crowd was hushed and given to kindnesses. As those in front had their fill of peering into the stable so typically nestled under the house, they quietly moved out of the way so others could see the sight. One after another moved forward until each beheld an infant, tightly wrapped in the clothes of a newborn, gently sleeping in a lamb's manger built into the walls of the stable. Fresh hay fell from the cozy bed and covered the floor, lending a sweet smell to the air.

Her legs suddenly felt weak, and she dropped to her knees, drawing Samuel with her. Tears coursed down her cheeks as Samuel raised the lantern to her face. "It is him," Samuel whispered in awe. It really is the Messiah." His eyes were wet with tears as well. She nodded. They stayed thus for several minutes, then, realizing others waited behind them, helped each other stand and moved away.

The light from his lantern seemed to change and grow brighter. Holding a hand to her eyes, she realized a pillow was under her head. Had she fainted? Rolling away from the light she realized she was in her own bed at home. At home? Heaving a long sigh of relief, she lay still, willing her mind to right itself. It had been a dream. Just a dream.

She considered what had happened, still immersed in the sounds and smells, feeling the wonder of it slipping slowly away.

Christmas, her Christmas, would never be the same.

The rush of the world came back as she noticed sunbeams coursing through her dirty window. The day was probably late for starting. With a sigh she pulled back the covers and swung her legs over the side of the bed.

Looking down, her heart did a little flip.

Her feet were caked with dirt.

21

CANDY CANE PRIZE

By Suzanne Baginskie

I remember the first holiday season we included our daughter Christine, age three, in the festive ritual of trimming the annual Christmas tree. While our favorite carols played on the radio, my husband wove several strands of yellow, blue, and red twinkling lights through the emerald-colored branches.

At first, she stared in awe and pointed at the tree, not comprehending why it was inside the tiny living room of our apartment. When we started hanging our favorite collection of shiny glass ornaments we gave a few to Christine. She dangled them on the tree's lower limbs and was so proud.

Soon, my husband carried in the stepladder. I did the honors of climbing to the top and setting the angel on the pine's highest peak. After it was adorned with a few boxes of silver tinsel, my hubby flipped the switch, and the sparkling began. Christine giggled and skipped all around the living room. Her small round eyes shone almost as bright as the tree.

Realizing I'd forgotten the box of candy canes tucked away in the pantry, I retrieved them and handed one to Christine to hang on the tree.

"Yummy," she said, and tried to rip off the wrapper.

"No, no. Don't open it." I took it from her and said, "These are very special candy canes to decorate the tree." I promised her after Santa's arrival she could have one. As a family tradition, we always waited till the actual holiday to eat them.

Christmas Day arrived. We had invited our relatives and friends to our home for the first big family celebration since my husband had been discharged from the U.S. Army during the summer. We would be having dinner together to make up for the previous couple of Christmases when we were many states away.

While I was preparing some special treats for the evening's menu, Christine shouted from the living room, "Mommy can I have a candy cane?"

"Not yet," I answered . . . but, too late.

A loud crash filled the air. Had Christine reached up and yanked one off? I rushed to the living room and found our stunned three-year-old, sitting amid the branches of the toppled pine tree. She clutched the peppermint-striped prize in her tiny hand. Her face glowed with triumph, but her button eyes were sober with fear.

"Sorry," she mumbled, and hugged me. I held her close and gazed at the fallen tree. It wasn't irreparably damaged, so my husband and I propped it back up.

While I cooked in the kitchen, he swept away a few broken glass ornaments, and straightened and rearranged the decorations the best he could. We may have had a slightly slanted tree, but everyone who came commented on how Christmassy it looked. I never said a word and made a mental note to purchase an extra box of small candy canes for Christine the following year.

Christine learned a valuable lesson that holiday. She never

grabbed at another tempting candy cane. In fact, recounting the tale of how she knocked over her first Christmas tree has become somewhat of a family tradition.

22

Markdown Angel

by Lydia E. Harris

One of my favorite Christmas memories began in a discount store.

As usual, I had hoped to buy nice gifts for my family. Yet finding something I could afford on that year's limited budget was a challenge. I prayed for guidance and felt nudged to try the new discount clothing store that had opened for the holiday season.

When I entered the shop, I noticed a box of sale items for one dollar each. I rummaged through it, hoping to find a bargain. Nothing suitable.

Farther inside the store, I found shelves of beautiful sweaters our teenage daughter, Anita, would love. The light-blue angora one with beads looked like her style. Perfect! I thought. I touched the soft sweater and glanced at the price tag — too expensive. I slowly put it back on the shelf.

As I headed to the door empty-handed, I glanced again into the discount box. To my surprise, a beaded light-blue angora sweater in my daughter's size lay on top. I examined it for flaws to see why it might be in that box. Perfect condition. Surely someone had dropped it in by mistake.

Showing the sweater to the clerk, I asked about the price.

"There's no mistake," she said. "It's one dollar."

What a find! I bought the sweater for Anita and thanked God for this bargain.

Our family's tales include a "markdown angel." Whenever we find an unexpected good deal, we say, "Oh, the markdown angel was here," meaning God provided something special for us. On the way home that day, I wondered if God had sent the markdown angel to lower the price for one certain shopping mom.

Once home, I carefully placed the sweater in a gift box and wrapped it in shiny paper, tickled with the find. On the tag I wrote, "To Anita, Love, God."

I couldn't wait for Anita to open her gift on Christmas Eve. As I expected, she loved the sweater. And I loved sharing why the label said, "Love, God."

We later took a family picture, with Anita wearing her angora sweater and all of us wearing big smiles. Whenever I see the photo, I am reminded that God loves to give good gifts to His children — perfect gifts.

That Christmas, we not only celebrated God's most precious and perfect gift of Jesus, we also rejoiced in His lovingkindness toward our family.

Every good and perfect gift is from above,
coming down from the Father of the heavenly lights,
who does not change like shifting shadows.

James 1:17 NLT

23

Gift of Hope

Suzanne D. Nichols

I breezed past the Christmas tree in my living room, almost upsetting one of its ornaments with the big, striped box I carried. *Slow down*, I told myself.

With only two weeks remaining until Christmas, I am certainly immersed in the holiday hustle and bustle. Today, however, an unexpected task has my full attention.

I've packed up a very old coat today. It's the same coat my Aunt Sarah wore in the 1950s while attending nursing school. The coat is knee-length now, but it was almost ankle-length then. That is, until the day my aunt got caught in the rain, and her mother — my grandmother — tried to dry it out over the floor furnace. Unfortunately, the heat scorched the lower portion of the beautiful cranberry-colored wool coat.

But being an industrious woman, and one not easily defeated, my grandmother made a straight cut high above the hem, removing all the burned fabric. She re-hemmed the shortened length and fashioned a button-on hood from the salvaged scraps. Although slightly redesigned, the coat's value was preserved and its purpose renewed simply because my grandmother saw promise among the ruins.

The coat was more than twenty years old when my grandmother gave it to me as a young newlywed. I'd not only needed a coat then, I'd also needed to see, through her reassuring example, that I could put my mistakes in the past and make the best of each day's new experiences.

Cherished memories flood my mind and I marvel at the significance this coat holds for me. Its appeal stretches beyond classic lines, lovely color, and warm fabric. My grandmother's vision and determination gave it an intangible quality more lasting and more valuable than the coat alone. I realize it has a story to tell, and the theme of that story is hope.

So, today, I packed it into a box. Not to store it away somewhere as a precious, untouchable keepsake but to let it go, to offer it a renewed purpose with a special young lady. I heard her say she needed a coat, and I instantly knew I could fill that need.

Although she is almost twenty years my junior, it's not difficult for me to see myself in her. A newlywed as I once was, she is learning and growing, determined to find hope in the trenches of her circumstances. She is now a wiser young lady, one willing to let God redeem the remaining value of a life scorched by wrong decisions. She is courageously allowing Him the freedom to cut away the ruins and redesign her, trusting His hands to stitch new life into what once represented defeat.

Settling into my car with the big, striped box on the seat beside me, I whisper a prayer for this young woman — the recipient of this sorrow-turned-solution gift. As I pray, I rejoice over yet another realization: The story of this coat is very much the message of Christmas. For in our hopelessness, God provided redemption through His Son. This Redeemer has come to reclaim scorched and ruined lives, to restore beauty and purpose, to bring victory out of sorrow and loss.

Put your hope in the Lord,
for with the Lord is unfailing love
and with Him is full redemption.

Psalm 130:7 NIV

24

Home for the Holidays

Laura Sweeney

I'm listening to concerts on NPR,
    (Chanticleer, the Tabernacle Choir on Temple Square)
while Freya Monster chunks out on German Stollen.

I check the mail for the first time all week,
    find three books, several bills,
and an envelope with red handwriting.

Back inside, I flip the letter over, tear the Smith stamp,
    open to find a postcard of a collie and a corgi,
red kerchiefs tied around their necks.

It's signed, "Happy Holidays, hope you're well."
    Well. It's been four years since our last squabble,
outside a restaurant in downtown Des Moines.

About my absence from my niece's graduation
    (the invite arrived late),
the Fourth of July party, the Labor Day event.

I wanted to be there, to see my sister's new décor,
    bohemian, art deco, or was it retro,
but I've not been able to clear the air.

I wonder, is she finally feeling our fragility?
    I hear she has an owl and a beehive,
and she's searching for retirement property on a Mexican beach.

Not much new here, just me and my dog Freya
　　　(whom in nine years she has not met)
enjoying this cozy soldier's cottage.

I've decided not to decorate,
　　　but I'm thinking to copy the single candles
in the window of the widow next door.

My neighbors' red berries look like velvet ribbons in their bushes,
　　　and the green moss and red leaves coiled around the trunk of my tree
remind me of construction-paper links.

Still, I'm eight hours away, no way to invite my sister to a house or dog party.
　　　I could tell her about my Hulu binge, one film about a girl with autism
and how she perseveres in independent living despite rejection,

estranged from her family,
　　　determined to submit a manuscript to a Star Trek contest,
something about Mr. Spock and coded emotions.

I could tell her I still believe in happy endings,
　　　like when her sister returns in the finale,
and the two cradle each other on the porch steps.

Or I could admit she was right about my ex,
　　　one reason I'm here living in precarity while my family of origin
toasts Tom & Jerrys, my grandfather's recipe,

or Dirty Snowmen, my brother-in-law's specialty,
　　　at her posh house in Des Moines.
The one I've never seen.

Instead, I opt to email a card, a jazz trio of snowmen,
　　　one playing the sax, her instrument.
"Cheers! Enjoy your toddies!"

25

The Jesus House

Bill Hufham

What we do sometimes speaks louder than what we say.

Several years ago, two or three days before Christmas Eve, my wife and I were sitting quietly in our living room, ready to settle down for the night. The fireplace was going and we were feeling cozy and warm. It had been a very cold day, and as night approached, the weather had turned freezing.

A knock came at our back door. When I opened the door, there stood a young, half-frozen teenage boy.

He had peddled his bicycle all the way from Wilmington, North Carolina to our house — over twenty miles. He said he wanted to see his girlfriend before Christmas, but he didn't have her address with him. He told us her name, hoping either my wife or I would know her since she lived in our area, but neither of us knew her.

After a few moments, he said, "Oh, I do have her phone number. Can I use your phone to call her?"

I said, "Sure you can use the phone, but let's warm you up a bit first. Come on in the house."

My wife gave him some milk and cookies and then told him to go call his girlfriend.

His girlfriend asked him where he was. Having seen our nativity scene in the front yard before he came up to the house, he replied, "I'm at the Jesus house. Do you know where that is?"

"I sure do. I'll be there in a minute to pick you up," she replied.

We do not call our home The Jesus House, but during the Christmas season, if you ask anyone in the area, "Where is The Jesus House?" they will direct you to our place.

Our nativity has a stable thirteen feet tall. Above it a large, six-pointed star reaches fifteen feet above the ground. The entire scene measures twenty feet wide. Everything is cut from plywood and all figures are life-sized. Every piece is painted a bright white.

We put up the nativity scene on December 1 and leave it up until after New Years Day. A light shines on it from 5:00 P.M. until 10:00 P.M. If you pass our house before 10:00 P.M. there is no way you can miss it — day or night.

26

Mary's Smile

Jeri McBryde

'm going to the ceramic shop. Want to come along?" Mom asked me.

"Why not," I replied. "What eighteen-year-old doesn't want to spend Friday night with their mother?

At the shop, I plopped down in a chair next to my mom and asked. "What are you making?"

"I'm working on one of the wise men." She held up the greenware. "I'm making a nativity set."

I looked at the table in front of us covered with small bottles of paint, strange-looking tools, and brushes. In the center stood the three wise men. Two were complete with elaborate robes and bearing gifts.

After a while, I walked around the busy workroom and admired the unfinished pieces of clay on the shelves. There were all types of pottery: bowls, dishes, cartoon figures, animals, music boxes, clocks, and vases. Then I saw them: wise men, camels, cows, donkeys, shepherds with sheep, and next to them, an angel and an empty manger. The Holy Family stood in center place.

I picked up Mary. The serene, loving look on her face touched me as I had never been touched. She was a young teenager, an ordinary woman, who had suffered. Her life was not easy, yet her smile enveloped me.

She was the bearer of all the traits a mother should have. She was conscientious, understanding, loving, and devoted to her child. I wanted to be just like her when I became a mother.

I went back to my Mom and held out Mary and her Baby. "I want to do these."

She handed me a cleaning tool and started explaining what she was doing.

* * *

Suddenly I was nineteen and married. It was Christmas. My own nativity set was finished just in time for our first Christmas. My new husband made a stable out of sticks and straw. Our first apartment was small. So was our tree. But Mary didn't care. She smiled as I placed her and the others under the Christmas tree.

Two days before Christmas I was in the kitchen when I heard a crash. I ran into the front room just in time to see our cat leap from the table where the Christmas tree stood. The wise men were scattered on the floor. My heart pounding, I gathered them up. They had survived. Catastrophe was averted. Christmas could go on.

Before we knew it, the Vietnam War was raging and my husband was drafted. Since I was pregnant, we decided it would be best if I moved back home. We had two nativity sets that year. Mom's was colorful and ornate with wise men in purple robes and jeweled turbans. My set was plain and simple, not painted, but stained the warm color of mahogany. I loved the way the stain gave it the look of hand-carved wood.

That Christmas I shared my fears with Mary — carrying my

first child, becoming a new mother, leaving my home, worrying about my husband. Mary knew how I felt. She knew about family and danger. She, too, had left her home, traveling to Bethlehem on a donkey, giving birth to Jesus in a stable. Her smile comforted me.

When our little girl was six weeks old, we moved to the marine base in South Carolina. We had a furnished two-room apartment. I took three special things with me: the baby, a crib, and the naivety set. I whispered to Mary about how scared I was to have the responsibility of raising my child far away from my family.

As we traveled in life, so did Mary, Joseph, and Baby Jesus. They have spent Christmas, under the tree, next to the tree, near the tree, on a counter, a tabletop, and now-and-then on a mantle.

Our small family grew to four with the addition of our son. Mary's suffering as she watched her son die on the cross hit home in a way it never had before. I knew the love a mother had for her children.

Over the years, our children would arrange the figures as we told the story of the Christmas miracle. Their small hands would gently cradle the Baby Jesus as they placed him in the manger. Someone broke a sheep, but Mary never told. She was good at keeping secrets. After all, she kept mine.

As the years flew by our tree became a big tree then a bigger tree. No matter the size of the tree, the wise men stood with their camels, the shepherds joined the sheep and a cow. The donkey looked out from the stable. Joseph stood by the manger watching over Mary and the Baby Jesus.

It's been fifty-six years now and Christmas has gone full circle. The children are grown and on their own. The Christmas tree is small again. But the nativity set remains the same . . . almost. It's worn in places, the cow has lost a horn, and a new sheep was added when the first was broken beyond repair. I couldn't match the color, so our newcomer looks a little out of place.

We have a new tradition now. I sit on the floor, take each piece from the storage box and hand them up to my husband. As I unwrap the precious cargo, I stop to read the old newspaper clippings that enfold them. The articles bring back memories, I reminisce about Christmases past. He stands patiently, waiting for the next figure to place on the fireplace mantle.

My husband always reminds me that the Baby Jesus is cradled in the underside of the manager. He places him there to keep the small figure from coming up missing next year.

Mary is the last figurine to take her place, next to the manger and the Christ child. The nativity set is complete, a reminder of what Christmas is all about.

I still share my fears, hopes, and dreams for my family with Mary.

She in turn gazes down upon us with her serenle, loving smile.

She brought forth her firstborn son,
and wrapped him in swaddling clothes,
and laid him in a manger;
because there was no room for them in the inn.

Luke 2:7 KJV

Unto you is born this day in the city of David a Saviour,
which is Christ the Lord.

Luke 2:11 KJV

27

Escort to Heaven

Del Bates

Suddenly, out of nowhere, Mom sat up on her own for the first time in twelve weeks. Not only did she sit up, but she also pointed to the corner of her hospital room and exclaimed, "Del, look!"

"What, mom?" I asked. What is it?"

"Don't you see her? She's right there?" she said.

I leaped from my chair and rushed to her bedside. "What is it, Mom? What do you see?"

As I turned around to see what she was pointing to, I glanced at the corner of her room, but all I could see in this age-old hospital room were the stucco walls and the stark white ceiling above.

"What, Mom? What is it?"

Her voice strengthened.

"Can't you see her, Del? She's right there!"

"What . . . what does he look like?" I asked.

Chuckling, Mom responded, "No silly, it's not he, it's she. She's standing right there. It's an angel."

Although I could not physically see any angel, I could not deny the warm presence that now filled Mom's room.

She lay back down just as still as she was before. Then minutes later she sat up with even greater excitement.

"Look, Del, she's back!"

I wish I could say I saw this angel Mom continued to speak about, but all I could see was the glow on Mom's face that mirrored its presence.

That evening, it was just me and Mom in her room. Usually, there was someone else there, too — one of my siblings, my children, nieces, or nephews — but as God would have it, this time we were there alone.

Three months prior, Mom had fallen and broken her hip. With one issue after another, her health continued to decline. Now, a few days before Christmas, the doctors explained to us that Mom was suffering from a severe infection in her back. As gently as possible, they let us know her time with us could be nearing its end. In a complete state of denial, each of us believed the doctors were wrong, and one day Mom *would* return home.

Yet that one evening, it seemed as though my mom had received a message from this angel. "Del, she said you need to go to each room and make the sign of the cross outside of each door. There are people right here on their way to hell. You must go and pray for them."

With her request, I knew these words were not from my mom; this was something the Lord wanted me to do. So, without hesitation, I went down the hall and prayed silently outside each room.

When I returned, I found mom fast asleep. I told her I had done as she requested. Although she did not respond — and never spoke another word again — I believe she somehow knew this mission was complete.

The next day I told one of our favorite nurses what had

happened. Although I didn't know how she would respond, I felt the need to share. To my surprise, she greeted me with a much-needed hug and words of comfort, "It's okay, Del, don't be alarmed. We have had many patients tell us about their angelic visitations just before they pass. That was the Angel of Death she saw."

Oh my Gosh! Was she telling me Mom had, indeed, had a visitation from an angel?

My eyes filled with tears as she continued to speak. "The gentleman in the very last room on the right was scheduled to go home for Christmas, but he passed away during the night. Because of what I have seen in the past, I believe this means your mom will be next to go."

Her straightforwardness left me speechless.

In God's way, He had spoken to each of my siblings and me about how Mom's Christmas present that year would be peace, and at her appointed time, He kept His promise.

On Christmas Day, the day on which Jesus whom she loved so dearly had entered this world, God sent an angel to escort Mom home.

Now, whenever Christmas rolls around, I not only remember it as the day our Lord and Savior was born, but also as *that* evening . . . when Mom received a visit from her personal escort to heaven.

28

Joseph's Christmas Night

Jean Matthew Hall

'm sorry, but this is the best I can do tonight." The innkeeper held the lamp up high. "Every room in the city is filled. We're packed! But there is clean hay. And the stable will keep the wind away and give you some privacy." He glanced at Mary's bulging stomach, then he put the lamp on a crate.

"Thank you. You are kind, sir," Joseph said. "We'll be fine."

"I'll send my boy out with some bread for you," the innkeeper said as he walked away.

Joseph raked dirty hay from the floor and dumped it into the ox's stall. He spread a deep layer of clean hay, then helped Mary down from the donkey and led her to the place he had just fixed for her.

She lay down and closed her eyes.

"*Ohhhh*," she moaned. She tossed and turned. Then she brought her knees up toward her chest.

"*Ohhhh!*" she moaned loudly.

"Another pain?" Joseph asked.

Mary nodded. "They are coming closer. It should be soon."

Joseph unloaded the donkey and tied him to a post. He unwrapped their bundle and spread out the things they had brought for the journey. They included strips of cloth for swaddling the baby. Mary had scrubbed them again and again to be sure they were clean for the little one.

"*Ohhhh*," Mary moaned again. "Joseph! It's time!"

He hurried to her side. She grabbed his hand and squeezed.

"*Ohhhhhhh!*" Mary took a deep breath and blew it out slowly. Then . . .

"*Waaaaaaaa!*"

A small cry told her the baby was here and healthy. Mary laughed and cried at the same time. "Let me see him," she begged.

"His lungs are strong and healthy," Joseph said. Mary nodded. Joseph wrapped him tightly in the clean cloths. He kissed the wrinkled face. Then Joseph handed the wailing baby to his mother.

"He's the most beautiful baby the world has ever seen," Joseph whispered.

Mary smothered the tiny face with kisses and spoke softly. "Shh, now. You're safe and sound." She held the baby close. Mary sang a lullaby her mother had sung to her many times.

Joseph scraped the sticky feed from the manger in the wall of the cave. He then filled it with clean hay.

"He's sleeping. Shall I lay him in the manger? You need to rest," Joseph said.

"Just for a while. He'll wake soon and want to suckle, I'm sure. And I want him close to me," Mary said. "I want to hear him breathing." She closed her eyes.

Joseph cradled the baby and laid him in the manger.

"Can you roll over, Mary? I'll put some clean hay here for you to sleep on."

Mary rolled over. Joseph pulled the soiled hay out and tossed it to the side. He scattered clean hay, then he spread his cloak on it for Mary. He helped her roll onto her other side. Joseph brushed Mary's hair out of her eyes. She smiled.

"I love you, Mary. And our new son, too."

"He is indeed special, Joseph." She took a deep breath. "Remember the angel?"

"Yes, I remember it all. *Shhh.* Rest now."

"You should rest, too. It's been a long journey," Mary said. She closed her eyes and fell into a deep sleep.

"I will, soon," Joseph whispered.

He walked to the manger and the sleeping baby. Joseph watched the tiny chest rise and fall, rise and fall. His little lips pursed and sucked.

"And you shall call his name Jesus," Joseph said out loud. "Lord, look what you have done! Such a miracle as this is unheard of. It's hard to grasp. I cannot understand how you can be this tiny, helpless baby and be Almighty God at the same time. Help me, God!" Then Joseph began to cry.

"Help me, God, to be his father on earth. Help me to protect him, teach him, guide him. How? How can I presume to do these things for *your* son?" Joseph turned and looked at Mary. "How can we be good enough to raise *your* son, God? This is too much! We don't know what we are doing. What if we teach him wrong? What if we make mistakes? What if we aren't smart enough? Strong enough? Good enough?"

Joseph fell to his knees. "God, Lord, what are we doing? What are *you* doing?"

With those words Joseph heard the baby cry.

Waaaaaaa! Waaaaaaa!

Joseph rose and walked to the manger. The baby hushed. He turned his little head and opened his eyes. Then he looked straight into Joseph's eyes.

The baby smiled.

Joseph smiled, too, as he reached down and picked up the child — the child God had given him to father, to guide, to train, to protect, to love.

Their eyes locked. Then this newborn baby cooed.

"I understand," Joseph whispered. "You'll help us, won't you?"

The baby smiled again.

"We're not smart enough, strong enough, or good enough. But you are. You are enough, Lord Jesus."

29

Gladys, and Her Father's Sacrificial Gift

Norma C. Mezoe

Gladys lived a few houses down the street from me in our small town of four hundred citizens. It wasn't until she had a need that we became acquainted. Al, her husband, needed transportation to a larger city for cancer treatments, and I volunteered to take them. This opened the door to becoming more than neighbors and we developed a close friendship.

Gladys was highly independent and remained that way until she was involved in an accident.

Another driver ran a red light and broadsided her car, which was totaled. She chose to stop driving at that time, and I became her designated driver.

Gladys had an unbelievable memory. In her nineties she quoted long poems she had learned in grade school. She had an inquisitive mind and an interest in the world around her.

One day she showed me an article she had written when she was much younger. Her writing expressed her concern for an alcoholic and the way he was shunned by neighbors. I encouraged her to write about other things that were of interest to her.

One day she showed me an article she had written about a gift her father gave her when she was a young girl. It seemed ideal for a magazine specializing in nostalgia. I submitted her story without her knowledge and it was accepted for publication.

It was with joy that I handed Gladys the published article, which included a picture of her as a ten year old. At the age of ninety-five, Gladys had become a published writer.

Following is Gladys' story.

It was Christmas Eve, 1929, and the depression was at its height. In addition to the hard times facing us, my family was also grieving the loss of my little brother, Junior, who had died in July.

Although I knew we were very low on money, I kept hoping there would be a Christmas present for me. When I was ready to go to bed, Mom said, "Gladys, you are ten years old and you know there is no Santa Claus. We don't have any money so don't expect a gift this year."

I pretended that I understood how things were, but after I went to bed I cried myself to sleep.

Sometime in the night I was awakened by the sound of our old truck pulling out of the driveway. I wondered where my father could be going on such a cold night.

I went back to sleep, but after a while I was awakened by my father standing by my bed. He handed me a book and said, "Merry Christmas, honey." I knew then that he had gone into town to our small general store and bought a present for me. I was so happy that I couldn't wait until morning to look at my book. When I glanced at the fly leaf, I saw PRICE: 25¢.

This happened in rural Sandborn, Indiana 83 years ago and I have received many gifts since then.

Each one has been appreciated by me but none will ever take the place in my memory of the one from a loving father who could only afford a twenty-five-cent gift.

Gladys was blessed to have a loving father. Many of us have experienced a similar love from our fathers. However, some children have never known a father's love. Perhaps their father abandoned them at birth and their mother struggled to provide a living. Some fathers abuse their children, verbally and physically. When Dad comes home reeking of alcohol, the children know to get out of his sight. They will never experience the love lavished on Gladys by her father.

But there is a Father who loves us unconditionally, no matter who we are or what we have done. We need not cringe in fear or hide from Him. God, our Father, loved us so much that He gave His perfect Gift so that we might have salvation and life eternal when we accept His Son as Lord and Savior.

Have you accepted God the Father's sacrificial Gift?

30

The Perfect Present Prank

Glenda Ferguson

I lifted the hefty paperweight out of the tissue paper in the sparkly paper box. The shiny dome reflected the colorful lights strung on the Christmas tree. A perfect present given to me by a prankster with a heart of gold that I would never forget. My friend Sharon has been gone several years, but she was uppermost in my mind. Even though she had been diagnosed with diabetes at an early age, the disease never limited her fun-loving personality. Sharon knew no boundaries to her faith. Her favorite verse was Philippians 4:13 (NIV): *I can do all things through Christ who strengthens me.* This year I vowed that her gift to me would not be stored away again. I would leave it on my table so that I could remember the good times all year long.

For several years, Sharon, her dad, and her mom hosted the Christmas party in their small house. Sharon and her family were some of the first friends I made when I moved to Indiana. Always included in any holiday celebrations were our other friends Karen, and Darlene and her young girls.

This particular year, their living room sparkled with decorations. The fragrant cedar tree, covered with all the ornaments in the family's collection, stood in the corner. Gold tinsel hung from the ceiling light fixture and extended to the four walls. Wrapped presents covered the floor. A soup pot full of spicy chili sat on the heating stove. Sharon served the crackers with spreadable cheese from a jar, which was popular every holiday.

The family dog loved all the attention . . . and the extra treats.

While we were eating, I noticed Sharon and her parents in a corner whispering. I might have been mistaken, but I thought I saw the prankster smile on Sharon's face. Almost like she was going to burst into giggles. However, as far as what I knew about Sharon, Christmas was off-limits for pranks. Birthdays, yes; she would mail one anonymous not-so-nice card that left you wondering who sent it, and in person, hand you a signed sentimental card.

Before I could alert our friends, Sharon and her parents were telling us about the display on the wall, over one hundred Christmas cards they'd received. In the dining room, her mom let us know which salt-and-pepper shakers were the most recent to join her collection of over one hundred pairs. Sharon showed us the dulcimer she was learning to play then strummed a Christmas song she had been practicing.

When it was time to open presents, Sharon set small gifts in front of my friends and me. Each box was carefully wrapped in sparkly Christmas paper with a matching nametag, and tied with a bright bow. I knew there was no way this was going to be a prank. I opened my box and searched through the layers of tissue paper. Finding nothing, I searched again. The box was empty! I glanced over at my friends. They were still searching. Sharon and her parents started laughing, which started all of us laughing.

"You got us," I said.

"The box and tissue paper are part of your present," Sharon

said. Her mom brought in a tray with a cloth covering. Sharon revealed each of our true gifts — a hand-blown glass paperweight. Red curved lettering was etched into the clear glass dome of mine: Merry Christmas Glenda.

There was no need to look at the monogram on the bottom. I recognized the craftsmanship of a local Indiana glassblower who was the third generation at his business.

These gifts took months of planning. Sharon must have traveled to the factory, met with the glassblower and selected just the right combination of colors.

We all thanked her repeatedly with words and hugs. What a thoughtful (and prank-loving) friend! When we were ready to leave for the evening, the hefty paperweights nestled perfectly in the tissue paper inside the sparkly wrapped boxes.

Until she passed away seven years later, Sharon experienced many health problems that limited her mobility. Her faith strengthened her even at her weakest moments. But every holiday my fun-loving friend celebrated with numerous cards, parties, and music.

That perfect Christmas present sits on my table so that memories of the prankster and the prank remind me of a strong faith all year long.

31

Homesick for Christmas

Diana L. Walters

We always spent Christmas at Grandma's house where aunts, uncles, and cousins gathered for a potluck meal. Afterwards Dad and his brothers played old-time country music on their guitars and banjos. Gram listened, her toes tapping, while Mom and the aunts cleaned up and gossiped.

I didn't much like that old music, so I escaped to my room with the girl cousins to talk about boys. Meanwhile, the boys went outside to build snow forts or play tag.

My father suffered a serious case of wanderlust. In the 1960s a machinist could find a job wherever he went, so Dad went — frequently. We moved nine times in my fourteen years, but we had never left Michigan, where he'd been born and raised as had generations before him.

Moving was a way of life for us, and we viewed it as an adventure. We never thought about what we left behind. We were pioneers going where our relatives had never gone.

Then one day Dad announced, "We're moving to Arizona. I'm sick of this cold. We're getting out before the snow flies."

"Yippee! We'll love Arizona," thirteen-year-old Donnie said. "I've heard it's summer all the time. We won't need our winter coats and we won't have to shovel snow."

The older boys discussed the fun of running barefoot all year long, while I envisioned sunbathing in the yard. Eddy, the youngest, listened with wide eyes.

It took some resourcefulness to pack a family of seven, but Mom was used to it. We children were too, and we knew the rules. We were each allowed to take three toys or non-essential items. Everything else would be given away.

I kept my journal and my two favorite books. My little sister, Sue, picked out her favorite dolls and a tea set. She begged to also keep the foot-long braid Mom had cut off when she gave her a pixie haircut. The answer was no; she had her three items.

We took time out from packing to attend a farewell party with the relatives. "You'll be back soon," Gram commented when I smuggled Sue's braid to her for safekeeping.

Dad and his brothers played music while the women visited. Aunt Judy said, "I can't believe you're going so far away," which caused Mom's eyes to moisten.

Uncle Bill tried to talk Dad out of moving. "What if you have a problem? You won't have family around to help."

Dad prided himself on his independence. He politely told Uncle Bill he didn't need anybody's help; he could handle anything that came up.

We set off in the old GMC Suburban, to which Dad had rigged a trailer of sorts and built something on top to hold as many belongings as possible. We probably looked like the Beverly Hillbillies, although we didn't take much furniture. We'd buy what we needed from thrift shops when we got there. Dad was a great thrift-shop negotiator.

He was also a great housing negotiator. When we arrived in Phoenix, Dad contacted a rental agency, dickered over the price (after all, he said, no one would be renting a place just before Christmas) and we moved into a 3-bedroom house.

The following Monday he'd secured a job and we were enrolled in our new school. We'd barely learned our teachers' names before Christmas break.

Our anticipation of running barefoot in the Arizona sun was thwarted by a yard full of sand burrs that stuck to the soles of our shoes and had to be pried off before we entered the house. Then there was the warning to watch out for scorpions and tarantulas.

As Christmas grew nearer, I began to think about the holiday preparations going on back home. We would have drawn names to exchange fifty-cent gifts with our cousins. On Christmas day we'd have enjoyed a potluck meal. Later there would have been music and laughter.

We'd always looked forward to the first snowfall of winter. That year we listened to "Santa's Comin' in a Whirlybird" on the radio and explained to Eddy that there wouldn't be any snow in Arizona. "Santa will come in a helicopter instead of a sleigh."

"I want snow!" Eddy insisted. I didn't blame him. It didn't seem like Christmas when it was sixty degrees outside.

On Christmas day, our family was unusually subdued as we ate our turkey, dressing, and mashed potatoes. Mom and Dad occupied a seat they'd removed from the Suburban while we sat cross-legged on the floor, our plates on top of packing boxes. We hadn't gotten around to buying furniture yet.

After the meal, Dad silently paced while the rest of us played cards. Donnie and Steve argued over the game, Sue and Eddy fought, and I felt weepy all afternoon. Mom's usual cheerfulness seemed flat.

I hadn't realized how much I'd miss our holiday traditions. I longed to feel my grandmother's plump arms hugging me and to taste Aunt Audrey's special casserole. I missed my giggling cousins. I even missed that old-fashioned music Dad and his brothers played.

A few days after Christmas Dad announced, "I don't like the weather here. We're moving back to Michigan."

We were all happy to return to our roots. I didn't think the weather had anything to do with moving back to Michigan, though. It was our home. There were people there who loved us. And despite Dad's declaration of self-reliance, he missed his family as much as we did.

The next Christmas, we gathered with aunts, uncles, and cousins at Grandma's house. We enjoyed a potluck meal of ham and turkey, sweet potato casserole, and a dozen other side dishes. Afterwards, Mom and the aunts cleaned up and Dad and his brothers played country music on their guitars and banjos. I enjoyed listening for a while before going to my room with the girl cousins. The boys went outside to build a snow fort.

It was a long time before Dad wanted to move again, and we were always home for Christmas.

After all, it was tradition.

32

My Names

Helen L. Hoover

While I was visiting our granddaughter Lacy, a few years ago, her two-year-old daughter, Lexy, persisted in calling me Mama, even when we told her my name was Grandmother. Mama was probably easier for her to say.

Actually, I was just tickled that Lexy talked to me. I really didn't care what name she called me.

Mrs. Hoover, Mother, Helen, Mom, Aunt Helen, Sweetheart, and Grandmother are all names that refer to me and describe my varied relationships with people.

I am happy to answer to any of them.

I'm reminded that God has many names. They describe His varied attributes. Some of His names are: Alpha, Omega, Holy One, Messiah, Prophet, Sovereign Lord, Rock of Our Salvation, Redeemer, King of Kings, Lord of Lords, Great Deliverer, Son of Man, Lamb of God, Lion of Judah, Christ, Anointed One, Savior, Good Shepherd, and Father. His names describe His wonderful relationship to His children.

As I am glad when people talk to me, God is also pleased when we talk to Him.

It is an honor to call upon Him and address Him by any of His names.

To us a child is born, to us a son is given,
and the government will be on his shoulders.
And he will be called Wonderful Counselor,
Mighty God, Everlasting Father, Prince of Peace.

Isaiah 9:6 NIV

33

The Magic of Christmas

Sue Rice

It was Christmas night and all through the house no creature was stirring except for one mouse. He ran to the tree only to see . . . he had somehow missed the big day!

How could that have happened?

Three tiny gifts were still waiting to be opened. The little mouse knew they were for him. He carefully unwrapped each of the presents. The first two gifts contained some of his favorite cheeses and a tiny scarf. When he was opening the third package, he noticed the little girl who lived in the house. Dressed in her pajamas, she was crying. He scurried to where she was standing.

"It is Christmas Day. What is making you so sad?" he said.

She looked at him through tear-filled lashes and sighed. "My daddy won't live here anymore. He has left my mother and me."

The mouse thought about that and asked, "Then what happens to you and your mother?"

The little girl heaved a great sigh. "We will have to go away too, silly. She does not have a job or jewelry she can sell to pay the rent on this big old house."

The mouse considered her plight and suggested she and her mother could live in his house with him and his family. "No one will notice if there are a couple more people and I will not charge any rent." The little girl smiled to herself as she considered his suggestion and promised to tell her mother of the generous proposal. She thanked the mouse and offered him a piece of her date-filled cookie.

As the mouse reached for the cookie, he slipped a scrap of paper into the little girl's hand. Then he returned to his house that was warm and cozy and always welcoming to those in need.

The little girl, still sleepy and heavy with grief about the situation with her mother and father, clutched the tiny paper in her hand and slowly made her way back upstairs to her room. Once there, she unfolded the tiny note and read it. Her eyes found the picture on her dresser of her with her mother and father. She sighed, gently touched the picture, and made a wish as she climbed back into her still-warm bed.

The next morning, as snow fell and smoke rose from the house's chimney, the mouse watched from his own home to see what might happen on this fateful day. The little girl's father had returned, the mouse observed, and he and the girl's mother sat talking at the round table near the kitchen window.

As the mouse watched, the girl walked into the kitchen and could hardly contain her joy at seeing her beloved father back home. She ran to him and hugged him and kissed his face. He looked at her with tears in his eyes. She smiled at her mother who looked as if she had suddenly become ten years younger.

That's when the little girl remembered the mouse's note and pulled it out of her pocket. Silently she read: "The magic of Christmas lies in the heart of a child." Now she knew exactly what that meant. She said a thank-filled prayer that God had answered her request, and that the mouse had spoken to her heart on Christmas Day when he knew a miracle might happen just like one had so long ago.

I Wish I Could Have Been There

Jean Matthew Hall

I wish I could have been there that dark and lonely night
when Jesus came into the world. I would have held Him tight.
I would have burped His tummy and counted all His toes.
I'd have let Him hold my finger. I'd have kissed His little nose.

I wish I could have been there to see Jesus' shining face,
to wrap Him in a blanket and make for Him a place.
I would have given my bed so He could rest His head.
I would have slept with the sheep in the barn instead.

But Jesus came long, long ago, and I am here right now.
I can only imagine His chin, His nose, His brow.
Though I could not be there that night so long ago
I see His face in others everywhere I go.

If I look in people's hearts and try to meet their needs,
I am touching Jesus with every thoughtful deed.
When I'm keeping others warm and seeing they are fed,
I can look into their eyes and see His eyes instead.

A Different Christmas

Barbara Loyd

We rushed to leave Baton Rouge early enough to reach our grandmother's house in Marksville, Louisiana before dark on Christmas Eve. Her little house had been ordered from the Sears & Roebuck catalog and built in 1935. My mother, brother, sister and I anticipated a fun time there despite the sad fact that this was our first Christmas away from our father. Our parents had separated six months before the Christmas holidays.

During our drive along the roads bordered by moss-hung oaks, my younger brother, Clyde, expressed his fear that Santa might overlook us since we were away from our own house. Mother, occupied with driving, did not answer him. I thought a few seconds then explained, "First, Santa will be attracted to Mama Jeanne's chimneys. Second, Santa's so smart he'll know where we are. Remember, he keeps track of all kids."

I sang a few words of the song, "He's making his list, and checking it twice, he's gonna know who's naughty or nice." My soprano white lies seemed to satisfy him. He relaxed in the backseat of our Chevy and didn't mention his concern again.

After we arrived and settled in, Mother announced, as she unpacked, "Oh, fiddle! I forgot to pack your Christmas stockings."

We improvised by hanging our extra socks above the fireplace in the living room. We toasted our backs at the cheerful, warming fire which our grandmother had started earlier to make us cozy.

Before long, delicious scents wafted from Mama Jeanne's kitchen. She rang her brass bell, which was shaped like a woman, then invited us to gather at her dining room table for a delicious dinner.

Bedtime arrived soon after we finished eating and we got ready to snuggle under the covers of the feather beds. My sister, Bettye, was sixteen; I was thirteen. We slept in the middle room. Its large wool rug — made from outgrown clothes — spread out over linoleum flooring that had been laid atop the wooden floorboards. This collage blocked out most of the cold air that seeped through the non-insulated floors from the crawlspace underneath the house.

Mother and ten-year-old Clyde would sleep in the front bedroom, which had a fireplace.

As we called out, "Good night, sleep tight, and don't let the bedbugs bite" to our mother and grandmother, we heard their laughter on the far side of the house in Mama Jeanne's bedroom. The mother and daughter were quiet as they rummaged around in the dark to find things to fill our three mismatched socks. I drifted off to sleep hearing the faint rustling of cellophane and tissue paper.

On Christmas morning, we squealed with joy to see that old Santa Claus had not forgotten us. While Bettye and I checked out the contents of our socks, Clyde stated solemnly, "Santa must have thought I had a tummy ache."

We craned our necks to see what he held up and gasped a

little to see a small, green-colored Tums package. His innocent belief in Santa touched us. I felt my throat tighten. Bettye and I exchanged glances and suppressed our giggles while Mother and Mama Jeanne scurried from the living room and headed for the kitchen. They could not confess their mistake of picking up the Tums, rather than mints, in the dark. Instead, they said, "We'll check to see if breakfast is ready."

Our happy mood continued after we opened our modest presents and finished the feast of French toast, fresh country sausages, and warm apple rings. Afterwards, Mama Jeanne turned on her black and white television in the living room. This did not happen often at our home in Baton Rouge. Mother did not allow us to watch TV until after we had finished our homework and chores. But because of the holidays, she relaxed her standards and laughed along with the rest of us at the festive, seasonal television specials.

Later, while Mama Jeanne played her upright piano, Christmas carols and hymns filled the little house. I claimed my favorite spot, hugging my grandmother's back, while she played and sang. On the old upright she managed to play *Jingle Bell Rock* twice. Our cousin Jim Boothe composed it with his friend Jim Beal. We all felt proud to sing his song. Another silly song we laughed and sang was *All I Want for Chistmas Is My Two Front Teeth*. Our grandmother claimed she could not play the even sillier *The Chipmunks' Song*, so we continued by singing *O Little Town of Bethlehem, Silent Night,* and other traditional songs our mother requested.

On Christmas Day Mother had always read Luke's account of Jesus' birth. That tradition continued this year and each following year, reassuring us that God protects and sustains us no matter what challenges occur.

My memories of our different Christmas linger because of the love and laughter our family shared despite the drastic changes in our lives.

36

Wishing You Many Christmas Sparks!

Vicki Indrizzo-Valente

My young mind was filled with imagination and stories of Santa with his reindeer upon the roof, floating down the chimney and landing, plop, right in the middle of our home. I believed and had faith in Santa, and lived the excitement of a child's Christmas.

All very wondrous.

As I reached adulthood Santa transformed from my childhood imagination and into my heart as my love for Christ.

Today, I feel something special each and every time I give someone a gift and say, "Merry Christmas!"

Tenderness fills my heart as I watch them open that gift they've wanted for so long. When I see it create a spark of joy and love in their eyes, I know they will cherish it for many years to come.

So, this is my gift to you . . . I wish you many, many Christmas Sparks and a very, very blessed and happy New Year.

37

The Whole Story About Christmas Blessings

Sandra Fischer

I t all started at Christmas time when I was eleven and heard Pastor Winters' sermon one Sunday. Pastor said, "If we're truly thankful for God's gift of His Son, we will share our gifts no matter how small. By doing so, we show the love of Christ and give God the glory. And we should share our gifts all year long because giving makes every day a celebration of Christ." Then, he asked us to bow our heads for the offering prayer.

Mama sighed and took a few small bills from her purse. I knew Mama wished she could give more. I tried to keep my head down during the prayer, but couldn't help peeking to see if Mr. Phillips would put anything in the offering plate this week.

Mr. Phillips was the owner of the general store where Mama worked. I thought he was the richest man in town. I reckoned he had lots of blessings and gifts to share, but I had noticed that each week the store owner handed the plate along when it came to him.

After the service, Mama and I filed out and Mama shook Pastor Winters' hand, thanking him for reminding us about sharing our gifts.

I asked, "Mama, do you think people here really have many blessings to share?" The small farming town we lived in had been hard hit by the drought that swept through Kansas, taking almost everything with it. It was a bleak harvest season. People could barely keep food on their tables, much less have anything extra to share.

"God always provides blessings, daughter, and we show our gratitude by sharing," Mama said. Mama had said that even after Papa died. "God blessed me with a job and gave you strength to help so we could keep our farm. Papa blessed others, too, by sharing our harvest and lending a hand when neighbors needed help. God blesses us to bless others."

Christmas came and went. We shared what we could with neighbors and friends.

After the new year something mysterious happened. People began receiving gifts out of the blue. Most were customers Mama chatted with at the general store. Folks would share a need with her and Mama would pray with them right there, asking God to provide. Within a week or so, packages containing just what those people needed would arrive from an anonymous sender. Attached would be an unsigned card that said, "Christmas blessings to you!"

Mama loved telling me the stories. "Nora Piper said her husband broke the ax handle he needed to chop wood. So, guess what came in the post today for Mr. Piper?"

"A hoe?" I grinned.

"Funny girl. And remember how Mrs. Winters needed a special brace for her bad leg, but they couldn't afford it right away?"

"Let me guess. The brace showed up at the store. Are you going to tell me God sent it?"

"Yes, I believe He did," Mama replied. "We just don't know

how, but He answered our prayers. Maybe Mr. Phillips knows. He sometimes hears us praying."

"I don't think it's Mr. Phillips," I told her. He doesn't ever put anything in the Sunday offering."

"How do you know that?"

"I see him just pass the plate."

Mama took my face in her hands, her gaze glued to mine. "Do you remember when Papa was sick, and we didn't know it? Remember how the doctor said afterwards Papa wouldn't go and get the medicine he needed, because we needed the money for seed? We didn't know how sick Papa was until it was too late because he kept it hidden. Sometimes, we don't know the whole story."

Mama wiped my eyes and hers with her apron. "God always provides," she said.

The provisions kept coming and Mama shared the stories every time. Homer Parker received a new harness for his plow horse after one broke. Millie Haller received three chickens to replace the ones a fox had taken. When Hannah Morris gave birth to twins instead of just one baby and needed extra clothes and formula, she received a big box full of just what Mama prayed for. On and on the provisions came long after Christmas.

The drought ended that spring when welcoming rain came to the thirsty land. Farmers planted new seed and the crops came in good measure. People thanked God for sending a good harvest and shared the blessings of it. Then, just before Christmas the accident happened. Mr. Phillips was unloading a wagon when one of the horses spooked. The wagon tipped over and fell on him, killing him instantly. It was an awful tragedy. I think Mama cried as much then as she did when Papa died.

Mr. Phillips' son, Wyeth, came for the funeral and Pastor Winters asked him to speak.

Wyeth told us how much his father loved and cared for him and his family and how generous he was. "My father was blessed. He made a small fortune in Topeka and wanted to share it. He bought the general store here, came to know you people and decided to stay. He said he could see God working in the hearts of people. Last year, he told me about Pastor Winters' sermon — how we should celebrate Christmas throughout the year by giving gifts all year long to bless others as we have been blessed. So, when he heard of a need, he would contact me and I'd send what was needed. But he never told anyone. He didn't want the credit. He said, 'God blessed me, so He should get the credit.' He always had me sign the card, 'Christmas blessings to you.' He even gave his tithe to the church in secret. He didn't want any praise or thanks to go to him. That's the kind of man he was. I share this with you today to honor him and to honor God, whom he loved and served."

I gasped and looked at Mama.

She smiled and squeezed my hand.

That's how I learned the whole story about sharing blessings and giving. Like Mama said, God always provides. He blesses us so we can bless others.

About the Authors

Becky Alexander loves all things Christmas, so participating in this book made her merry and bright. It's her third Christmas book; she contributed to the Divine Moments' *Christmas Stories* in 2020 and *Coffee and Cookies with God: 31 Devotions for December* in 2021. She volunteers year-round with Operation Christmas Child, a ministry of Samaritan's Purse.

As a devotional writer for Guideposts, Becky's work appears in *Mornings with Jesus 2023* and *Pray a Word a Day*. Her story "Connected by Kindness" in *Chicken Soup for the Soul: Miracles & Divine Intervention* received first-place awards from Carolina Christian Writers Conference and Southern Christian Writers Conference. Connect with Becky at HappyChairBooks.com.

Suzanne Baginskie retired from a 29-year career as an office manager/paralegal in a law office. She has sold several short mysteries, romance stories, and over 20 non-fiction stories to *Chicken Soup for the Soul* books and *Cup of Comfort*. Her first published book, *Dangerous Charade*, Book One in her FBI Affairs series, was released in October, 2021. Book Two, *Dangerous Revenge* is now out.

Her short stories appear in *Behind Closed Doors* anthology, *A Heart Full of Love* collection, *Woman's World*, *Plan B Mystery Magazine*, *The Wrong Side of the Law*, two *Daily Flash Fiction* volumes, *Woman's World Magazine*, *First Magazine*, *True Romance Magazine*, *Guideposts*, *Futures Magazine* and *Turbulence & Coffee*. She is a member of MWA, FMWA, Sisters-in-Crime, and The Short Mystery Fiction Society.

Visit her website at: http://suzannebaginskie.webador.com.

Del Bates is an author, speaker, and an enthusiastic encourager. She has been in leadership with Aglow International for many years. She has self-published two books and has numerous stories in various publications. Her latest book on Spiritual Warfare, *Walking in a Minefield* was released in June of 2021.

Del and her husband are snowbirds, dividing their time between Florida and Michigan. In Michigan she spends quality time with her three-adult children, their families and finds plenty of time to spoil her five grandkids. Contact her at Delbates.com.

Susan Brehmer, an encourager and Bible enthusiast, believes treasure is found in the Word of God, and time with Jesus sheds light on Scripture. She loves to lead others into worship and through the life-changing Word of God.

Susan supports her fellow travelers on their trek through the Bible and had fun crafting a ten-minute summary of the Old and New Testament as a souvenir of their journey together.

Susan is host of the *Encouraging Voice Podcast*, writes worship songs, and her devotions have been featured in *Pathways to God* and *Guideposts*. She likes to create profoundly simple ways to approach and read the Bible to connect with the heart of God. Bible resources, helpful hints, motivation, and encouragement can be found at www.SusanBrehmer.com.

Joann Claypoole, the award-winning author of *The Gardener's Helpers*, is a wife, mother of four sons, "Numi" to four grandchildren, and doggie-mom of two.

Her numerous articles and inspirational stories with multiple publishers include Grace Publishing's Selah Award-winning *Divine Moments* series, Bethany House, Baker Publishing Group, and most recently, Guideposts books. In addition to blogging at *Dreamdove's Flights of Fancy*, and guest blogging at *The Write Conversation*, she's a long-standing monthly blog contributor at *Inspire A Fire*.

This Melanoma survivor and former spa-girl entrepreneur now prefers to write, explore mountain trails, and invite deer and other wildlife to stay for dinner near her western North Carolina cabin. Connect with her via FaceBook, Instagram, LinkedIn, Twitter, and her website.

Jennifer A. Doss resides in Indiana with her husband and four children. Each day, she strives to draw closer to God and find ways to inspire and encourage others. Her other joys include spending time outdoors in the shade and hanging out with her family. She credits any success or achievements to the Lord and gives all credit to Him.

Rhonda J. Dragomir is a multimedia creative who treasures her fairy tale life in central Kentucky, insisting her home is her castle, even if her prince refuses to dig a moat. She has published works in several anthologies and periodicals, and is seeking publication of her first novel, an historical romance. Visit her author website: www.rhondadragomir.com.

Glenda Ferguson graduated from College of the Ozarks in Missouri and Indiana University with education degrees. After retiring from teaching reading and fourth graders, she started writing. She now contributes to *All God's Creatures, Angels on Earth, Chicken Soup for the Soul, Reminisce* and *Sasee.* The Indiana Arts Commission has included her poem "The Buffalo Trace Trail: Then and Now" into the INverse Poetry Archive. Glenda receives encouragement from writers at the Burton Kimble Farm Education Center and the Prayer Circle at her church. During the holidays her husband, Tim, decorates the outside of their southern Indiana home with numerous light shows.

Sandra Fischer is an Indiana retiree who lives in Southern Pines, North Carolina. Her first book, *Seasons in the Garden,* filled with inspirational prose and poetry, compares the seasons of nature to human life. Her second book, *My Faithbook Messages*, is a devotional, and her third book, *Every Day Is Christmas,* is filled with heartfelt Christmas stories illustrated by artist friend, Becky Guinn, who paints with a mechanical arm.

You can find a list of Sandra's books on her Amazon author page: https://www.amazon.com/-/e/B00ISC2GA4.

Constance Gilbert writes inspirational short stories. Music and books have been a major part of her life since age 7. She knits and colors to stimulate her little gray (brain) cells, but studying Scripture is her passion. Connie, a retired RN uses her many experiences plus the nearby Cascade Mountains and three grandkids to inspire her. Connie's most recently published story, "Olivia, the Fierce," shows her love of taking everyday things and happenings to a deeper level.

Jean Matthew Hall lives in LaGrange, Kentucky with her old-lady dog, Sophie. Jean writes poems, stories, articles and picture books while Sophie naps. Her first picture book *God's Blessings of Fall* was released in September 2019. Her second picture book is set to release in 2022.

When not enjoying time with family (eight gorgeous grandkids) and church, Jean is immersed in children's picture books — reading, studying, reviewing, and writing them. Jean has been a Christian for more than 50 years.

Jean is a member of the SCBWI, Word Weavers International, Write2Ignite and the Kentucky Christian Writers.

You can learn more about Jean at her website and blog www.jeanmatthewhall.com. Find her on Face Book at Jean Matthew Hall Author and on Twitter at Jean_Hall. Check out her Boards on Pinterests at JeanMatthew_Hall.

Bonnie Lasley Harker, mother, grandmother and great-grandmother, loves God, her family and her poetry. She says poetry came to her as a gift from God during a time of pruning, as spoken of by Jesus in John 15:5. However, the gift has continued for 23 years, and includes devotionals.

She never knows when inspiration will come. She testifies to the fact God triggers it with a couple of phrases, and leaves the rest in her hands. May He be glorified forever.

Lydia E. Harris has been married to her college sweetheart, Milt, for more than 50 years. She enjoys spending time with her family, which includes two married children and five grandchildren ages 12 to 23. She is the author of two books for grandparents: *Preparing My Heart for Grandparenting: for Grandparents at Any Stage of the Journey* and *In the Kitchen with Grandma: Stirring Up Tasty Memories Together.*

With a master's degree in Home Economics, Lydia creates and tests recipes with her grandchildren for Focus on the Family children's magazines. She also pens the column "A Cup of Tea with Lydia," which is published in the US and Canada. It's no wonder she is known as "Grandma Tea."

Helen L. Hoover and her husband are retired and live in the Ozark Mountains of southern Missouri. Sewing, reading, and knitting are her favorite pastimes. However, caring for the flower and vegetable gardens and helping her husband with home projects receive priority on her time. She treasures visits with their children, grandchildren and great-grandchildren.

Helen is thrilled to be included in 27 compilation books. Word Aflame Publishing, Word Action Publicating, *The Secret Place, The Quiet Hour, LIVE, The Lutheran Digest, Light and Life Communications, Chicken Soup for the Soul,* and *Victory in Grace* have published her devotionals and personal articles.

Bill Hufham, an accomplished writer and artist, has published over 600 articles as a weekly contributor to *The Columbus Record*. He is sought after as a Christian speaker and often does chalk talks for churches and civic organizations.

Linda L. Kruschke writes candid memoir and fearless poetry, and delves into hard issues others avoid. She blogs at *AnotherFearlessYear.net* and *AnchoredVoices.com*, and has been published in *Fathom Magazine*, *The Christian Journal*, *Bible Advocate*, *iBelieve.com*, *WeToo.org* blog, *The Mighty*, *Calla Press*, and several anthologies. She is editor of *Swallow's Nest*, the poetry journal of Oregon Christian Writers.

Barbara Latta, a true southerner, is a transplant from Arkansas to Georgia. She writes a monthly column in her local newspaper and contributes to devotional websites, online magazines, and has stories in several anthologies. She is the author of *God's Maps, Stories of Inspiration and Direction for Motorcycle Riders*. She enjoys traveling with her Harley-riding prince on his motorcycle taking in the creativity of nature. Drinking coffee on the patio at sunrise is her favorite time of day. Barbara shares about walking in grace and thriving in hope on her blog, *Navigating Life's Curves*, at www.barbaralatta.blogspot.com. She cherishes her role in life as a wife, a mom, mother-in-law, and Mimi to one granddaughter.

Barbara Loyd, graduate of the University of Maryland in 1974, majored in Art History and Literature. During her career, she taught art to students in grades 1-12, and adults. A studio painter, she uses vivid color in her award-winning art which has been displayed locally, nationally, and internationally. As an author, she also aspires to be colorful in her published writings and poetry. Her husband and two pets liven up Barbara's life in Granbury, Texas.

Jeri McBryde loves sharing her life experiences in the *Chicken Soup for the Soul* series with the hope of helping others. Her stories have appeared in nine of the series' books. Another of her stories was published in Divine Moments' *Remembering Christmas*. Her works also appear in three additional anthologies.

Jeri lives in a small southern-delta town. Retired, she spends her days reading and working on her dream of publishing a novel. A doting grandmother, her world revolves around faith, family, friends, and chocolate.

Bonita Y. McCoy hails from the great state of Alabama where she lives on a five-acre farm with two dogs, two cows, four cats, and one husband who she's had for over 32 years.

She is a mother to three grown sons and a beautiful daughter-in-law, who joined the family from Japan.

She loves God, and she loves to write. Her articles, devotions, and novels are an expression of both of these passions.

On any given day, you can find Bonita photographing flowers, reading a sweet romance or a cozy mystery, or chilling on her front porch swing.

She is an active member of both American Christian Fiction Writers and Word Weavers International.

Drop her a line at bonitaymccoy@yahoo.com or sign up for her newsletter at www.bonitaymccoy.com.

Margaret McNeil is a wife, mother and food writer. She lives with her family and their rescue cat in Memphis, Tennessee. She loves to cook and entertain. You can find recipes and cooking tips on her website margaretsmorsels.com.

Norma C. Mezoe has been a published writer for 37 years. Her writing has appeared in books, devotionals, Sunday school take-home papers and magazines. She is active in her church in a variety of roles. Norma became a Christian at the age of 15, but didn't grow spiritually in a significant way until a crisis at the age of 33 brought her into a closer relationship with the Lord. Norma may be contacted at: normacm@tds.net.

Margaret Nava writes from her home in New Mexico where she lives with a rambunctious Chihuahua and writes inspirational articles for Christian publications. She has authored two books about New Mexico, one about West Virginia, and three "Lady-Lit" novels, all available on Amazon.com.

Suzanne D. Nichols grew up in Gulf Breeze, Florida where, during a high school composition class, she discovered the rewarding discipline of writing. Through the years, she has found creative expression in almost every genre of the printed word. She especially enjoys blending words and art in ways that can both delight and challenge the observer.

Suzanne, a 2021 Selah Awards recipient, is published in seven books of the *Short and Sweet* series, a co-author of *COFFEE with God* Volumes 1 and 2, a contributor to *Day by Day: 40 Devotionals for Writers & Creative Types*.

Suzanne makes her home in Hartselle, Alabama with her husband of 46 years. They have three children and 10 grandchildren who live much too far away.

Theresa Parker Pierce lives in historic Salisbury, North Carolina, where she enjoys spending time with family and friends. Theresa has a Master's degree in education and is National Board-certified. She has 35 years of experience teaching reading and history. Two-time Rowan Salisbury Teacher of the Year, Theresa enjoys storytelling and giving tours.

A historic docent, she splits her volunteer time between the North Carolina Transportation Museum in Spencer and the

Rowan Museum in Salisbury. With what started as one but is now a closet full of costumes, Theresa dresses in period attire.

A Toastmaster, she speaks to historic groups, senior citizens, and of course, her favorite children.

Sue Rice, a Kent State University graduate, is retired from a career in Human Resources Management. She enjoys writing and has been published in a number of magazines including *Guideposts*, *GRAND*, and *The Liguorian*. A current ESL teacher, Sue has worked with students from around the world.

She enjoys hiking with her dog, Buddy (They have logged over 1,000 miles.). She is working on a book about people's memories of spending time with their grandmothers.

Beverly Robertson, a retired elementary school instructional aide, earned an associate degree from Delta College in her later years. She networks and hones her writing skills as a member of American Christian Fiction Writers. For her Presbyterian women's group, she presented lessons on different women of the Bible. Beverly authored the book *Bible Brides: Trials and Triumphs*. She lives in Michigan and is married with a daughter, stepson, five grandchildren, and four great-grandchildren.

Carol Smithson has been creating stories, poems, and plays from the time she could write. She promised herself that when she left nursing she would take up writing as her retirement profession. Since January, 2021 she has written a kindle book, *Grandma's Space Camp,* and is currently working on a fictional drama, *Accused,* and a musical, *James.* This is her first contribution to a Christmas anthology.

Pamela Stein is an elementary school librarian in a school for dyslexic students. She is a writer, photographer, scrapbooker, and paper artist. She writes children's books, middle grade books, devotionals, poetry, and memoirs. Pamela has been published in professional library journals, local publications, and Grace Publishing's Christmas anthologies. She is a member of the Bartlett (Tennessee) Christian Writers group and on the board of the Mid-South Christian Writers Conference. She is currently working on board books, a picture book biography, a middle grade novel, and a book of devotions based on the Psalms.

Laura Sweeney facilitates Writers for Life in Iowa and Illinois. She represented the Iowa Arts Council at the First International Teaching Artist's Conference in Oslo, Norway. Her poems and prose appear in more than 60 journals and 10 anthologies in the US, Canada, Britain, Indonesia, and China.

Her recent awards include a scholarship to the Sewanee Writer's Conference. In 2021, she received an Editor's Prize in Flash Discourse from *Open: Journal of Arts & Letters;* Poetry Society of Michigan's Barbara Sykes Memorial Humor Award; and two of her poems appear in the anthology *Impact: Personal Portraits of Activism,* which received an American Book Fest Best Book Award in the Current Events category, and finalist in the Social Change category. She is a PhD candidate in English/ Creative Writing at Illinois State University.

Donna Collins Tinsley, wife, mother, grandmother, and great-grandmother, lives in Port Orange, Florida. Her work has been included in several magazines and book compilations. You can find her on Facebook, at http://thornrose7.blogspot.com/ or join Somebody's Mother Online Prayer Support Group on Facebook. You may email Donna at thornrose7@aol.com.

Vicki Indrizzo-Valente has always loved transforming her thoughts and faith into words through poetry, music, and short stories. It stems from her teenage years, romance and adventure, up to the present life lessons of being a senior. She lives in Mystic, Connecticut where she has settled for her retirement, just hoping for some more time to write. Her published works include "My Love," in the *Lindenhurst Bulldog* newspaper, "Who Am I," in *The Hatchet*, and "My Family Has Found Its Own Definition" in *Grace Magazine-Life Stories*.

Diana L. Walters lives in Chattanooga with her husband. Together they develop ministry materials for people with dementia. At age 74, she continues to work part-time enriching lives at a retirement community. She gardens and writes in her spare time. Diana has been published in *Chicken Soup for the Soul* books, *Upper Room* magazine, and other devotional publications.

Divine Moments

If you would like to read more faith-filled stories like those in *The Christmas Spirit*, you'll love the other books in this series, available through your favorite online retailer or on our website: grace-publishing.com.

Grace Publishing Anthologies

If you're a writer with a story to tell, consider submitting your work for inclusion in upcoming books in a Grace Publishing anthology.

Divine Moments

Divine Moments is an award-winning series. Each book is a labor of love, so no one is compensated monetarily. Authors share with the possibility of changing someone's life, heart, or mind. All royalties from this series go to Samaritan's Purse, an organization that helps victims of war, poverty, natural disasters, disease, and famine with the purpose of sharing God's love through His son, Jesus Christ. However, each of the authors whose work is selected to be published will receive a free copy of the book and a discount on orders.

Send your personal articles! The story is the important thing. The article length is anywhere from 500-2,000 words. Previous books have included poems and even some pieces written by children, so the guidelines aren't strict. The main point is the context of the story. (Take a look at previous Moments books that Grace Publishing has released, particularly the first one, *Divine Moments,* for examples.)

Both multi-published and beginning or non-published authors write for the series. Stories may be original or previously published if rights have been returned (as long as we are informed of the latter in advance). Grace Publishing retains rights after acceptance until publication, then rights automatically return to the author.

Submissions should be Times New Roman, 12-point type, sent as a Microsoft Word attachment to an email. Subject line should include the title of the book. Please include in the header at the top of the submission: your name, mailing address for the one free copy, your email address and the story's word count. Also include with your submission a bio of 100-125 words. Each writer's bio will appear in the About the Author section at the end of the book. Send to Terri Kalfas: terri@grace-publishing.com.

Divine Moments Is Accepting Submissions for the Following Titles for 2023-2024

Lost Moments: These can be funny stories of just being "stupid" while others may be very serious, like not trusting or believing God; may be the loss of a relationship, a friend, or loved one; or may be humorous stories of losing one's eyeglasses while they're sitting on your head, or losing one's train of thought or someone's name (serious or humorous).

Questionable Moments: Whether these stories are serious or funny, they should be the "What was I thinking?" type of story. They might even address whether the questionable behavior was redeemed or even redeemable, and why or why not.

Favorite Moments: Personal stories of times that bring a smile to your face whenever you think of them, and will make others smile, too.

Divine Detours: Stories that show how your personal plans/goals/actions were changed because of God's movement in your life, the way you responded during the experience, and when or how you realized God was in control and "behind" it all.

Unexpected Kindness: These should be stories of a time in your life when you received unexpected or undeserved kindness/grace from others.

Patriotic Moments: These stories go beyond the typical school essays from childhood. They are stories of actions that exemplify true personal love and celebration of the U.S.

Hopeful Moments: These stories should be uplifting. They can include (but are not limited to) what hope and hopefulness means to you, seasons of hope you have experienced, and stories of times when all hope seemed lost until. . . .

Christmas 2023 and Christmas 2024 (both as yet untitled)

Short and Sweet Series

Each book in the *Short and Sweet* series is a labor of love, so no one is compensated monetarily. Authors share with the possibility of changing someone's life, heart, or mind. All royalties from this series go to World Christian Broadcasting, a non-profit organization whose purpose is to take God's Word — through mass media — to people who may have no other means of hearing the Good News. However each of the authors whose work is selected to be published will receive a free copy of the book and a discount on orders.

For this book series we use words of only one syllable in the stories related to the book's theme.

Seven exceptions to the one-syllable-word-only requirement:

1. Any proper noun is okay. (If you were born in California, don't write Maine; if a name is Machenheimer, don't write Clark.)

2. You may use polysyllabic words of 5 letters or fewer — for example: into, over, area, about.

3. You may use contractions of more than one syllable such as couldn't, wouldn't, didn't.

4. You may use numbers (even those that are polysyllabic).

5. As in any published work, direct quotes — even in casual conversation — must be rendered word-for-word as they occurred, so their wording is exempt from the rules. This includes verses from the Bible — but only translations, not paraphrases (such as *The Message*).

6. Multi-syllable words for family (for which there are no single-syllable synonyms) are fine: mother, father, family, sister, brother, sibling, husband, daughter, relative etc.

7. Words for which no synonym exists — such as college/ university, heredity, communication, integrity, honest/honesty, person, regret, career/ profession, passion, destination, hospital, education/ teacher/professor, institution, creativity, identity — or that cannot be replaced by a natural-sounding phrase of simple, one-syllable words.

Writers often find it easier to write the story, then go back and replace the words that don't meet the series' requirements.

The general purpose of your piece is to entertain — rather than to teach or merely inform — so the tone should be personal and optimistic rather than instructive.

Both multi-published and beginning or non-published authors write for the series. Stories may be original or previously published if rights have been returned (as long as we are informed of the latter in advance). Grace Publishing retains rights after acceptance until publication, then rights automatically return to the author.

The article length is anywhere from 250-1,000 words. Previous books have included poems. The main point is the context of the story. (Take a look at previous *Short and Sweet* books that Grace Publishing has released.)

Submissions should be Times New Roman, 12-point type,

sent as a Microsoft Word attachment to an email. Subject line should include the title of the book. In the header at the top of the submission, include: your name, mailing address for the one free copy, your email address and the story's word count.

Please include with your submission a clear, crisp, 300 ppi/dpi color headshot (as an attachment in jpeg format) and a a bio of no less than 100 and no more than125 words. Each writer's photo and bio will appear in the About the Author section at the end of the book.

Send to Susan King: shortandsweettoo@gmail.com.

Short and Sweet Is Accepting Submissions for the Following Titles for 2023-2024

What Patriotism Means to Me: These stories might include topics like: How your patriotism connects with/reflects other deeply held beliefs. How you live your life differently because you are patriotic. What you consider the duties/rights of a patriot. How your views about (or feelings of) patriotism might have changed over the years. What you have taught your children about patriotism. (If you have you taught primarily by example, how?) If you learned about patriotism as a child, what was the source?

Mishaps and Misadventures: Vacations that took an unexpected turn along the way. These stores are about your best and funniest vacation memories, created by something completely unplanned.

Memorable Mutts

The Feline in the Family

Facing Fears: Facing and conquering fears big or small, whether as a child or an adult.

CPSIA information can be obtained
at www.ICGtesting.com
Printed in the USA
LVHW080338241122
733963LV00016B/1345

9 781604 950854